The Second Commandment

D1566048

The Second Commandment

Loving Your Neighbor in Today's Changing World

BY Joey R. Peyton

FOREWORD BY
James Littles

WIPF & STOCK · Eugene, Oregon

THE SECOND COMMANDMENT
Loving Your Neighbor in Today's Changing World

Wipf & Stock
An Imprint of Wipf and Stock Publishers
199 W. 8th Ave., Suite 3
Eugene, OR 97401

www.wipfandstock.com

PAPERBACK ISBN: 978-1-6667-8820-4
HARDCOVER ISBN: 978-1-6667-8821-1
EBOOK ISBN: 978-1-6667-8822-8

VERSION NUMBER 01/23/24

This book is dedicated to the two people who, with the help of God, changed my life more than any other: my beloved wife, Karen L. Peyton, and Joseph Charlie, a Yupik Eskimo who taught me how to daily live the second commandment, and, after finding God's beauty together, went on ahead to be with our Lord and Savior, Jesus Christ.

Then one of them, which was a lawyer, asked him a question, tempting him, and saying, "Master, which is the great commandment in the law?" Jesus said unto him, "Thou shalt love the Lord thy God with all thy heart, and with all thy soul, and with all thy mind. This is the first and great commandment. And the second is like unto it, Thou shalt love thy neighbour as thyself. On these two commandments hang all the law and the prophets."

—Matt 22:35–40

Contents

CONTENTS

List of Illustrations

List of Tables

Foreword

After a lifetime dedicated to learning and growing as a disciple, I think I have come to some decisions on what makes a great book for me. Great books start with authors who know what they are talking about. I benefit the most from authors who have seen a need and dedicated themselves to many cycles of study and application. This kind of wisdom takes years to bear fruit. The author invites you to trace their journey and join with them in their next steps of missional faithfulness.

As a reader I want to be challenged without being demoralized. Unless I am reading for leisure after a busy season of labor, I need my books to be meaningful in a way that makes me a better disciple of Jesus. Joey Peyton checks all these boxes in his current book, *The Second Commandment*.

I first met Joey when he came as a midlife student to Urshan Graduate School of Theology over twenty years ago. Since then, we have transitioned from the professor and student relationship to becoming friends and colleagues. Through the passing years I have observed the personal and professional growth from those early explorations of the twin commandments to the current work that presents both the depth and breadth of what it means for twenty-first century disciples to love God and neighbor.

Peyton writes with a personal, direct style that flows from decades of service as a missionary, pastor, teacher, evangelist, consultant, and advocate for those overlooked due to cultural blind spots or deep sins of rejecting people because they are different or unimportant. If you must have a paint-by-number approach to discipleship that always ends with accepted measures of success, then this book is not for you. If, on the other hand, your heart has experienced both God's lavish, undeserved love and intense pain of seeing a world that suffers from untold dimensions of brokenness, then this book will serve as one of God's tools to help you in the next step of growth.

As you read though *The Second Commandment*, you will be gripped by the Good Samaritan-like opportunities in everyday life around you. Peyton carefully collects biblical, theological, historical, and sociological data to develop a model of second commandment ministry that can be applied to needs you encounter every day. Peyton carefully applies the second commandment method to pastoral care, Christian education, Christian counseling, time of death, and immigrant care issues. He infuses personal engagement examples in each area of loving neighbor. His humble transparency rests on simple faith that Jesus' birth in Bethlehem set the stage for reconciliation, peace, and hope for all humanity. That same faith causes him to conclude his book with the words of Jesus, "Go and do likewise" (Luke 10:37).

I give thanks to the Lord for the volume you hold in your hand. I have anticipated Peyton's completed project from those early days when he wrote papers for my Mission of the Church class at Urshan and then returned to teach the course himself. The refining process of two doctoral degrees, additional service to the church and academy, and personal commitment to getting his hands dirty while caring for neighbors in need have given Joey Peyton the moral, spiritual, and intellectual right to produce this transformative book.

I pray each reader hears the biblical call to love God and neighbor in fresh, new, personal ways. I pray for the reader's spiritual strength and personal courage to faithfully respond to the call. I pray for fresh waves of God's grace as readers become conduits of that grace as they love others in Jesus' name.

Christmas Day 2023
James A. Littles, Jr., Ph.D.
Professor Emeritus
Urshan Graduate School of Theology

Acknowledgments

It would be completely dishonest to not acknowledge the wealth of support and assistance that I have received in the writing of this book.

First and foremost, I must acknowledge the role of the Holy Spirit that has walked with me in this rather lengthy journey. The words, "Loneliness! Stark, relentless, loneliness! Empty, pointless, purposeless lives filled with loneliness . . ." found in chapter 2, were first written in 2002 at the beginning of my graduate-level education journey. The revelation of the second commandment was God's answer to the loneliness that I had lived with my whole life. Two graduate degrees and two post-graduate degrees later, the revelation of the Bible's command to love one's neighbor has been the driving force of every endeavor and the answer to my loneliness. The more I studied, the more God's Holy Spirit has revealed himself and the importance of loving one's neighbor in my life and the life of the church. Each line of this book has been the Holy Spirit poured out through this earthen vessel.

Second, this book could not have been written without the encouragement and love-of-neighbor extended to me by my wife, Karen. In 1991 she picked up this broken vessel and three very broken children and lived daily, for the last thirty-plus years, the ministry of the Good Samaritan. Not only was she committed to loving this neighbor selflessly, from the shores of the Bering Sea to the potato fields of Northern Maine, and to the highways across our world, but she also brought gifts to this ministerial union that have made this book possible. She has proofread every word, every chapter, every paper, and every version that has ever been written. She has discussed, researched, preached, taught, and prayed about every theological point and every scripture utilized. Her gift of the English language refined the lack of such skills for this man from the cornfields of Southern Illinois. Her ability to stand toe-to-toe and vehemently discuss the correctness of the eternally confusing elements of proper punctuation, grammar, and layout expectations, made all of this possible. I am forever indebted to her for her love and for making this project of more than twenty years feasible.

Transparency demands a final acknowledgement of the academic institutions that tolerated, encouraged, and, to some degree, embraced my passion for the love of neighbor: Wayland Baptist University that encouraged me in a life of learning; the Urshan Graduate School of Theology for laying the groundwork for a life of theological research; Eden Theological Seminary for expanding me with an understanding of the human need for pastoral care; and the Assembly of God Theological Seminary for expanding on my love for learning, my love for the Bible, and my love for humanity with an understanding of the complexities of culture, the mission of God, and the ever-changing world of God's creation. Each school played a vital role in who I am today and my understanding of the joint-love commandment (love God, love neighbor).

From the bottom of my heart, I am thankful to my God, my wife, and to all of my professors and their institutions. Without any of them, this project would not have been what it is today. "Thank you" seems completely inadequate, but it is all I have. So, for all those who will read these words and love their neighbors, I say "thank you," . . . in eternity, the least thanks you . . . and the God who made and loved the world thanks you for helping me teach others to love their neighbors.

List of Terms

Christian Counseling	(pastoral counseling) covers a wide range of counseling techniques and methods, but all are based upon the principles of (and a belief in) the Bible.
Christology	the study of Christ (as God incarnate).
Common Era	commonly known as AD (anno domini—in the year of our Lord).
Diaspora	forcefully displaced immigrants.
Ekklesia	(Greek) the church, an assembly of people.
Emulate	to learn, achieve, or be successful based upon the imitation of another.
First/Second Commandment	"Jesus said unto him, Thou shalt love the Lord thy God with all thy heart, and with all thy soul, and with all thy mind. This is the first and great commandment. And the second is like unto it, Thou shalt love thy neighbour as thyself. On these two commandments hang all the law and the prophets" (Matt 22:37-40).
Imago Dei	(Latin) image of God

Joint-love commandment   love God, love neighbor

Modern Pentecostal Movement   early twentieth century Pentecostal outpouring.

Neighbor   (*plesion*—Greek) one who is nearby (proximity).

Narrative   the use of story to explain our needs, feelings, and theology.

Pastoral/Pastoral Care   pastoral care refers to a full range of care/ministry provided by the church for the body of Christ (the church is that body) and for their neighbors/community.

Praxis   practice or custom that comes from a real belief in . . . (e.g. Christopraxis)

Second Commandment Ministry   When exposed to others by proximity, the second commandment is a commandment that commands the practical demonstration of one's love for his/her neighbor(s), down to the least of them, loving them as one does him/herself, that springs forth from the depth of one's love for God.

1

Introduction to the Second Commandment

And the second is like, namely this, Thou shalt love thy neighbour as thyself. There is none other commandment greater than these.

—MARK 12:31

Sally never went to church on Sundays; in fact, seventy-eight-year-old Sally never went to church at all. She had no friends that remained alive, and her extended family rarely visited. Therefore, her days were lonely and empty, each one blended together until they all seemed to be the same. She had few reasons to leave her home because her fixed income only allowed for the purchase of a few groceries after the rent was paid. Her neighbors, Jim and Sharon, were much younger, and they had little in common with Sally. She did watch them as they left for church three or four times a week. The family looked so clean, healthy, and happy!

To the people around them, Jim and Sharon seemed as if they had the world by the tail. They went to First Church at least three times a week and were faithful supporters of the church. However, Jim worked sixty to eighty hours a week, and Sharon was often left alone to raise the kids. Because Sharon was tied down with raising three kids and keeping a house that competed with the others in her church, she had little time to entertain, fellowship, or attend the ladies' meetings at First Church. Her church friends were also busy and did not have much time to share or visit. Jim and Sharon did not fight a lot, in fact everyone thought they were very much in love, but they just seemed to drift apart as the lonely years swept by.

On the other side of Jim and Sharon were some of those "welfare" people, moved in by the local welfare office. To Jim and Sharon all they ever seemed to do was produce more kids. Jim and Sharon could not keep up with the number living there, neither did they know the names of the children or the parents. Jim and Sharon often considered buying the run-down house next door to be able to prevent a bad influence on their children and increase their own property value. However, the best that they could afford to do was to no longer allow their children to play outside until they could build a six-foot privacy fence around the backyard.

If the welfare neighbors were not enough of a blow to Jim and Sharon's neighborhood, rumors were going around that the government was selling empty houses to Guatemalan refugees. Now, even if they were interested in reaching their neighbors, their new neighbors couldn't speak English well enough to communicate, and someone said they didn't even speak Spanish. Many of their customs were strange, and Jim was told at work that one family was seen roasting what looked like a goat over an open fire in the backyard. The small-town schools were already overcrowded, so where did they expect to go to school? Especially with language barriers, cultural barriers, employment barriers, and so much more impeding the education process?

Jim and Sharon's pastor, Pastor Levi, pastor of First Church, appreciated having faithful members like Jim and Sharon in the church because they required little maintenance and were faithful in both attendance and financial support. Pastor Levi was troubled with how to find a way to teach Jim and Sharon, and others like them, many of the truths of God's Word, for which two or three services each week did not provide enough time. Things like, "How do I get Jim and Sharon involved in some kind of ministry?" or "How do I get Jim and Sharon to witness to their neighbors?" While it was good to have low-maintenance saints, Pastor Levi knew little about them, their backgrounds, or their talents. Consequently, Pastor Levi had no idea of the pastoral care they needed and, because of their stability over the years, he assumed they didn't need any care at all.

Furthermore, First Church had never really grown a whole lot since it was started seventy years ago. The church had run between fifty and seventy for the last fifty-plus years. It was so frustrating to see each year go by with the addition of one or two and the loss of one or two. Many a night Pastor Levi stayed awake wondering how to get people like Jim and Sharon involved in helping First Church grow. One hot summer day, Pastor Levi was especially glad Jim and Sharon didn't need any care because "old" Fred was finally dying. He had no idea what to do when he visited the nursing home with all of Fred's family standing around the walls of the room. If that wasn't enough, nine people from Guatemala were in church on Sunday, and it seemed none of them spoke English. As pastor, he felt forced to try out his high school Spanish, and they acted like they didn't understand a word he said. What was he supposed to do when Fred died, and what was he going to do with the Guatemalans if they came back next Sunday?

Over the years Pastor Levi had tried many different programs but had eventually grown tired of all the efforts with little or no results. In fact, he became so passive that he had learned to just be thankful for great people like Jim and Sharon, whose contributions kept the church going and required no pastoral care. You can imagine the shock when one day Betty, Fred's daughter, a faithful member of First Church and a secretary where Jim worked, called Pastor Levi to inform him that there were rumors at work that Jim and Sharon were getting a divorce. On further investigation, Pastor Levi found out that Sharon was at home packing boxes and was moving back home to live with her mother until she could get back on her feet. How could this happen? Pastor Levi spent hours sitting at his desk with his head in his hands asking the questions, the same kind of questions so many other pastors asked each week: "Where did I go wrong? How could such a stable couple suddenly decide to get a divorce? Why am I so surprised? Was it too late?" And if those weren't enough, new questions seem to arise every day. "What was he supposed to do when Fred died, and what was he going to do if the Guatemalans came back next Sunday?"

WHILE THIS STORY IS fictional, it has been fabricated from the many true stories experienced during the years of most pastorates and becomes a potential reality from which to explain the principles of living out the second commandment in the life of the church. Furthermore, these composite stories, and others like them, are happening every day throughout the Christian world. The pastoral questions, "Where did I go wrong?" and "What could I have done differently?" will be addressed in the light of the second commandment. The mistakes/solutions will be expanded beyond Jim and Sharon to encompass many other areas outlined in the story above. The reader will see that the problems created by an absence of love for others impact the ministerial efforts of every pastor, the ministry of every church, and the lives of every child of God. The question is often asked, "What could one do, and would the efforts be too late or ineffective?" It is hard to tell exactly when it is too late to try to help someone, but one thing is sure: if one continues to do nothing, there is little hope for Jim, Sharon, Sally, Fred, the "welfare" family, the Guatemalans, and the church in general. Therefore, let us collectively turn our attention to exactly what this book will cover for the reader.

In the first section of the book (chapters 2–5) an explanation will be given of the second commandment (to love one's neighbor) with an emphasis on a biblical and theological understanding. Chapter 2 will undertake a biblical examination to explore the words of Jesus, "Thou shalt love the Lord thy God with all thy heart, and with all thy soul, and with all thy mind. This is the first and great commandment. *And the second is like unto it, thou shalt love thy neighbor as thyself.* On these two commandments hang all the law and the prophets" (Matt 22:37–40).[1] The relationship between the first and second commandments will establish a foundation from which to understand God's joint-love commandments (love God and love others). Foremost, the intention of this book is to show the difference that second commandment ministry could make in the daily lives of churches like the one described above. By examining one's responsibility to live out the joint-love commandments, the reader will begin to understand the impact such modified behavior will have upon the church and her larger community.

Further, Luke 10:25–37 (the joint-love commandments and the Good Samaritan story) exists as the example for the early church to emulate Christ while living as his body in their first-century world. Therefore, chapter 2 will also consider how the early church embodied the second commandment (loving one's neighbor) in her fulfillment of the first commandment (loving God). As a result of living out both commandments, Christianity spread, first to her neighbors, and then around the world. This will demonstrate that today's church cannot separate the first commandment from the second commandment but will show conclusively that loving one's neighbor is a demonstration of one's love for his/her Savior.

Chapter 3 demonstrates the practical application of the second commandment in the life of the church today by examining the early church in

---

1. All Scriptures are from the King James Version (KJV) unless otherwise indicated.

the New Testament. What would the church community look like if many Christians would love their neighbors in the same way they love themselves? Could the second commandment help save a marriage? Could its impact save lives, comfort the dying, and welcome the stranger? If Christians lived the life envisioned by Christ when he first spoke the words of the first and second commandments, what might be different? Can loving one's neighbor really minister to the poor and lonely? Could the second commandment help fill up empty church buildings? What would the church look like? How would the people act? What would be required of the church if it behaved like Jesus and the apostles of the early church? These questions will be addressed throughout this chapter, while describing a biblical definition of second commandment ministry. The main point in this chapter will be to join what the Bible says with what the church does!

Chapter 4 will examine how the early church emulated Christ and took on the very characteristics of his ministry on earth among the very least, specifically because they understood him to be the Son of God. Because of such emulations, early believers were called Christians (Christ-like) and the church existed as his body to reconcile the world to the Father. If the world is to recognize the church as Christ's body today, the church will have to live the second commandment, acting like Christ among the very least, the very poor, and the stranger. It is when humanity sees the church being the church, a church that, like Christ, has God-like characteristics, they will believe on/in Christ and glorify his Father which is in heaven. The point of this chapter compels the church to follow Christ, who lived out the second commandment every day. The same Jesus instructed the disciples at the last supper, shortly before his death, "For I have given you an example, that ye should do as I have done to you" (John 13:15).

In chapter 5, the existence of the second commandment will be examined in Modern Pentecostal movements (1900 to present). Is the expansion of Pentecostalism from a handful in 1900 to over five hundred million adherents today attributed solely to the infilling of the Spirit, or does it owe some of the revival to a secondary source? This chapter will demonstrate how that in many cases the greater the emphasis was placed on the second commandment, the greater the spread of the Pentecostal phenomena. Further, can an absence of the second commandment extinguish all hope of a Pentecostal presence in some areas, even if the leaders are Spirit-filled? The history of the modern Pentecostal movement shows that pastors must do more than be filled with the Spirit if they want to grow beyond the average thirty to fifty in attendance. They must present the Pentecostal experience with the love of Jesus Christ to a lonely world in the arms of the second commandment.

In the second section of the book (chapters 6–10), the second commandment (love of neighbor) will be applied to the many pastoral roles in the church. Chapter 6 will demonstrate how the second commandment is foundational to the pastoral care provided by the pastor and church. Pastoral care, orchestrated by the pastoral leadership, is the care provided by the church for the church (and community).

Chapter 7 explains the second commandment's impact on the overall Christian educational experience. Christian education is often empty and meaningless unless it is modeled so that others can imitate it. Further, modeling and imitation is enhanced by the second commandment; with meaningful fellowship one can model the second commandment lifestyle, which, when seen by others, can then be easily imitated. Some of the greatest lessons ever taught have been caught/understood by one's example in a home during everyday fellowship.

Chapter 8 demonstrates how Christian counseling, a practice still greatly feared by many, is increasingly acceptable when offered in the embrace of the second commandment. Often, Christians avoid counseling when offered in an office with a given appointment time. However, many will willingly receive godly counseling, howbeit sometimes unwittingly, over a cup of coffee or a game of horseshoes. Few people respond well when confronted in an office, but most will hear the words of a friend that loves them. The collective pastoral role of the church, as a community of believers, should be dedicated to the encouraging and building up of one another.

Chapter 9 will show how the second commandment prepares the way and provides comfort to the grieving at the time of death. No ministry is more painful and more difficult than ministering before, during, and after the death of someone loved by the church. In the embrace of one loved by their neighbor, grief can be understood, the future can be faced, and the hope of eternal life be promised.

Chapter 10 lays out principles for living the second commandment in intercultural settings. While race/ethnicity often divides community, the commandment to love one's neighbor mandates that the church must be different. The church today is faced with differences of color, gender, age, culture, citizenship, language, and/or place of birth; however, the church is led by the God who sees all, loves all, and cares for all. A second command-ment church can do no less than emulate the God they serve.

Finally, in chapter 11, a summary of the second commandment will compel the reader to live and practice the principles of the joint-love com-mandment (love God and love neighbor). As well, the final chapter will suggest further areas that need research, application, and understanding. While the reader can go to the specific area of the book that interests them, a better understanding of the overwhelming biblical evidence for loving one's neighbor while loving one's God can be achieved by reading the first section before jumping into one of the specific areas in the second section. This author's prayer is that this book will encourage a multitude of believers to love their neighbors, love their enemies, and to love all, no matter how different, how strange, or how much they do not like them.

—— SECTION ONE ——

Biblical and Theological Support
(Chapters 2–5)

All scripture is given by inspiration of God, and is profitable
for doctrine, for reproof, for correction, for instruction in
righteousness.

—2 TIM 3:16

What does the Bible teach us about the second commandment?

AT THE VERY FOUNDATION of everything that Christians believe is the
biblical record. It is important to this author and, hopefully, to the reader
to establish the second commandment as encompassing the Scriptures
from Genesis to Revelation (*chapter 2*). Further, the early church's behavior emulated the behavior of Christ as they lived out the mission of God
(*chapter 3*). The acceptance of Jesus as God, and their understanding of
God as one, resulted from how Jesus lived the mission of God during his
ministry on earth (*chapter 4*). Finally, the modern Pentecostal movement,
that spread throughout the world in the early 1900s, blossomed in the
hands of the church that loved both God and their neighbors (*chapter 5*).
When Jesus was asked what was the greatest of the commandments, Jesus
said, "Thou shalt love the Lord thy God with all thy heart, and with all
thy soul, and with all thy mind. This is the first and great commandment.
And the second is like unto it, Thou shalt love thy neighbor as thyself.

On these two commandments hang all the law and the prophets" (Matt 22:37–40). In another place Jesus reminded them, "If ye love me, keep my commandments" (John 14:15). This book is written to those that love Jesus and compels them to keep both commandments; love God with all you are and love your neighbor as yourself.

Section One—The second commandment and . . .

- Chapter Two—Biblical Foundations
  (What does the Bible Say?)

- Chapter Three—The Church
  (What should the church do?)

- Chapter Four—Early High Christology
  (How did they know Jesus was God?)

- Chapter Five—Modern Pentecostal Movements
  (How has love produced revival?)

2

The Second Commandment and Biblical Foundations

Master, which is the great commandment in the law? Jesus said unto him, Thou shalt love the Lord thy God with all thy heart, and with all thy soul, and with all thy mind. This is the first and great commandment. And the second is like unto it, Thou shalt love thy neighbor as thyself. On these two commandments hang all the law and the prophets.

—Matt 22:36–40; Mark 12:28–34; Luke 10:27–37

Pastor Levi knelt, as he did many mornings, at the altar of the church before he started his day in the office. There before him, his Bible was opened to the story of the Good Samaritan. The final words of the story seemed to jump out at him, "Go, and do likewise" (Luke 10:37). If only he had the time to be the Good Samaritan, but he had to figure out what to do about Jim and Sharon. "God . . . " he pleaded, "I need Jim and Sharon. I need their faithfulness, their attendance, and yes, Lord, I confess. The church needs their money!" The words of his morning devotions seemed to echo in the empty auditorium, "Go and do likewise!" "But God," he tried to explain, "I must go see Fred before he dies . . . I have sermons to prepare, the offering to count, and the toilet in the men's room is not flushing! I need to brush up on my Spanish! God, I don't have time to be the Good Samaritan!" As he knelt there a few more minutes, his loneliness was magnified by being alone in a building built for one hundred and fifty people. He

> *wondered why he had never been able to find an assistant pastor to help him do the things he needed to do. "If I wasn't so alone, I might be able to go and do like the Good Samaritan." Pastor Levi continued to pray, "God, I have too much to do, and I am so lonely . . ." and yet the voice of God spoke from his written word, "Go and do likewise!"*

LONELINESS! STARK, RELENTLESS, LONELINESS! Empty, pointless, purpose-less lives filled with loneliness! Wandering the crowded halls of society (even among the people that will sit next to you in church this Sunday), Americans are the loneliest people in the world![1] From the mega-malls to the high-rise apartment buildings, there has never been a time in Ameri-can history that America has been more crowded; yet, at the same time, Americans continue to be among the loneliest people in the world. Crowds of one hundred thousand that used to be a novelty are now so common that they rarely make the headlines. Pushing through these crowds are millions of lonely people. Lonely people that are spending millions to talk to people that they've never seen, on the phone, the radio, and in internet chatrooms. In the mental health field, which was in its infancy prior to World War II, psychiatric medicine and psychotropic medication have be-come a multibillion-dollar industry serving millions of lonely Americans, always searching for something to fill the lonely void.

Over one hundred years ago, America embraced the Western doctrine of individuality, and our individuality has spawned loneliness and isolation-ism. Individuality has not been isolated to people outside the church but has permeated throughout all of Christianity, from the pulpit to the pews and from Catholics to Pentecostals. A common Christian slogan at the end of the twentieth century was, "Me and Jesus got our own thing going." Ameri-cans are not just going to the grocery store and the post office alone; they are going to church alone, sitting on the pew alone, and going home even more lonely, wondering at that empty, unfulfilled feeling that goes with them throughout their lonely lives. America has drive-thru fast food, drive-thru cleaners, drive-thru pharmacies, and now we even have online churches where one can drive-thru even more alone than ever. Such individualism and isolationism are not isolated to the pew but may be even more prevalent in the pulpit and the parsonage. Christians claim to know God and to love him, yet something is very wrong with this picture.

1. Frazee, *Connecting Church*, 24.

The Christian world has become very comfortable with the first commandment (at least as far as it is understood) that commands one to love God with all her heart, all her soul, and all her mind (Matt 22:37). The modern church worships God with great exuberance: sometimes including running, leaping, and shouting for joy at the knowledge of (and love for) God. Christians often feel blessed beyond measure with the revelation of truth and the hope of salvation. The church has utilized their understanding of God to justify worshiping until they literally drop in exhaustion from the effort. However, many still go home to a long, lonely week, waiting for another weekend service to give it all they've got for another couple of hours. All week long many churchgoers wonder about the emptiness of the week and the loneliness of the nights.

This limited view of the first commandment (loving God), to the complete exclusion of the second commandment (loving others), does not fulfill the commandment to love God. The result of isolating one's love for God from one's love for others is loneliness. Rather, loving God can only be completed when actively loving the world he created. "If a man say, I love God, and hateth his brother, he is a liar: for he that loveth not his brother whom he hath seen, how can he love God whom he hath not seen?" (1 John 4:20). At the same time, fully loving one's neighbor is only possible because of the love we have found in Christ Jesus.

One must consider what the second commandment means from a biblical and a practical perspective in the lives of the church today. This relationship between revival and the joint-love commandment (loving God and loving neighbor) must be examined if the church is to understand the path to revival and the fulfillment of the kingdom of God. The lack of revival and/or the blessings of God's kingdom here on earth are often related to the absence of a practical love for others. The Bible teaches that the love of God is fulfilled by obedience to the command to love others, even one's enemy (Luke 6:27, 35). Full obedience to this joint-love commandment will greatly impact the twenty-first-century church community, and the need is urgently felt in our day.

A Christian World Without the Second Commandment

One of the biggest mistakes of modern Christianity is to equate church with a building or a location. Long before the first building, the church existed in an upper room and the first outpouring of the Holy Ghost spilled out into the street (Acts 2). One of the first words to describe the church was the Greek word *ekklesia,* which refers to an assembly of people. It is important to note that *ekklesia* was never used in the New Testament to refer to a building or place. The term *ekklesia* was used three ways in the New Testament. First, *ekklesia* was used in a secular sense meaning an assembly of people (Acts 19:32). Second, *ekklesia* was used to refer to the Israelites in the wilderness (Acts 7:38). Third, and by far the largest with over one hundred references, it described a group of believers without regards to a building or a geographic location. Stephen, instructed and ordained by the apostles, taught, "the most High dwelleth not in temples made with hands" (Acts 7:48). The apostle Paul followed up with a similar discourse when he asked the question, "Know ye not that ye are the temple of God, and *that* the Spirit of God dwelleth in you?" (1 Cor 3:16). The people are God's tabernacle in this world; the people of God are the place where hungry souls can find comfort and food.

The point, the church is not a building but rather an assembly of people (believers), is well proven; unfortunately, many Christians would describe the church (or a church) as a building. This leads to a major obstacle to daily living the second commandment and, at the very least, creates a limit to where the church must obey the command to love their neighbors (only at the church building). This explains why many Christians are satisfied with doing church on Sunday morning, and a few, more fanatical, Christians might attend church three times a week. Some consider this paying their religious and/or social dues, and the rest of the time is theirs to do with as they see fit. When only two to six hours out of a long week is applied to going to church, this leaves a huge vacuum in which people do many good things but almost never intentionally loving others. This extremely small weekly contribution to the first commandment allows the church to ignore the second commandment for the rest of the week.

Even though Christians spend two to six hours together each week, most of this time is spent in organized worship and teaching or preaching, thus attempting to fulfill the command to love God. This allows, maybe, ten minutes per service (before and after the church service) in which to establish relationships and to love others; thereby fulfilling the second commandment. It is no wonder that Christians struggle to remember the names of the people with whom they attend church. Divide these few minutes each week among a church of one hundred regular attendees, and they have about ten to thirty seconds to love each person. With only seconds to be friendly and obey the second commandment, very few bother. Solomon exhorted, "A man that hath friends must shew himself friendly" (Prov 18:24). However, with no time to be friendly, even with fellow Christians, many Christians have few Christian friends. As well, because of the way they have been taught, most have few friends outside their church, which also limits the ability to love others. The bottom line is that many Christians are lonely, and, consequently, some may even be lonelier than their un-churched counterparts.

> To even the most casual observer, the loneliness experienced by Sally was probably no different than the loneliness that consumed Sharon and Pastor Levi, who attended three church services a week.

It can be argued that few can faithfully serve God for any length of time without a community of believers that love and care for each other. Human beings are social beings and will look to satisfy the lonely void in their lives. Boy Scouts, Girl Scouts, clubs, billiard halls, gangs, schools, colleges, the military, and even prisons are all forms of community. Jim Bakker reflects that, despite eighty-six services each week at the last church he pastored at Heritage USA, it was not until he went to prison that he really learned about Christian community. "It was there—in prison—that I experienced the best Christian community I had ever known."[2] People join a community, or become part of one, to be able to belong to something that fills the lonely spots in their lives.

> It's no wonder that Sally and the welfare family were not attracted to church by observing the lonely behavior of Jim and Sharon. Further, it is doubtful that the Guatemalans, who are seeking a welcoming community and friendship in their new American home, will find it from a pastor who himself is lonely. Fred will most likely die lonely, like many, and his daughter will wonder who will fill the lonely void caused by the death of her father.

Community outside the body of the church springs from a personal and social life that is infected with self-centeredness and individuality. Not being a part of something creates an emptiness that constantly desires to be

2. Baker and Abraham, *Refuge*, 37.

filled by the temporary pleasures of the world. Many times, young people leave the church because they do not feel like they belong nor are a part of what the church is doing. They want to belong; they want to have owner-ship; they want to have a part; and they want it to be relevant and mean-ingful. This loneliness drives millions of faithful churchgoers of all ages to divorce, to barrooms, to parties, and to gangs in a desperate attempt to find the community and the love not available within the church.

Looking at the church world from a broad-brush perspective, we find that there are generally two kinds of churches in our world today. The first kind of church is a first commandment church, and their motiva-tion is strictly in worshiping and loving God, but they often avoid loving their neighbors. The second kind of church is a second commandment church, and their focus is social welfare (loving their neighbor), but often they avoid the kind of commitment and belief in God that comes from loving God. The important thing to note is that both principles are well-founded in the Bible. What is needed in the Christian world today is more churches that pursue principles of both the first commandment and the second commandment in the life of the church and, by extension, into the least of the church's surrounding community.

Foundations of the Second Commandment

The Relationship of the Two Commandments

One cannot fully understand the command to loves one's neighbor unless she/he understands the relationship between the two commandments. The first commandment requires that one, "love the Lord thy God with all thy heart, and with all thy soul, and with all thy mind" (Matt 22:37). However, at first glance this passage does not give practical instructions on how to love God with all the heart, soul, and/or mind, and it seems that loving God is left for individual interpretation. Consequently, one hears a wide variety of answers that range from total obedience to God to a total absorption into the things of God. When looking across Christianity, one will find that some people have walked on coals of fire, crawled on streets strewn with broken glass, danced for hours to the point of exhaustion, hung from crosses, attended all-night prayer meetings, abandoned the world, and many other things when attempting to love the Lord with all their heart, mind, and strength.

However, the Bible does not leave loving God to one's own interpretation, and neither is it as hard to understand as some may think. Quite the contrary, the simple way to love God is in obedience to the second commandment, which is like the first, "love thy neighbor as thyself" (Matt 22:40). Jesus cleared up any questions when he explained why the faithful would go to heaven: "Come, ye blessed of my Father, inherit the kingdom prepared for you from the foundation of the world: For I was an hungered, and ye gave me meat: I was thirsty, and ye gave me drink: I was a stranger, and ye took me in: Naked, and ye clothed me: I was sick, and ye visited me: I was in prison, and ye came unto me" (Matt 25:34–36). The righteous were astonished and replied with the question, when did we do any of these things? (Matt 25:37–39). Jesus' reply here mirrors the principle behind the second commandment, when he tells the righteous, "Inasmuch as ye have done *it* unto one of the least of these my brethren, ye have done *it* unto me" (Matt 25:40). In this passage Jesus directly connects loving the least with our efforts to love him. If one desires to love God with all his heart, soul, and mind, the way to do this is by obeying the command to love one's neighbors (even the least of them). Jesus knew how subjective the first commandment would be for people limited by their humanity and provided a second commandment that is "like unto the first" by which to understand it (Matt 22:39).

Contrary to what some may think, the command to love God is very specific with two very important principles. The first principle details what must be done when loving the Lord with all your heart: love your neighbor. The second principle explains how to love one's neighbor: lovers of God must love their neighbor in the same way they love themselves. For only when one loves his neighbor as himself is he truly loving the Lord with all his heart, soul, and mind. Jesus explains the punishment and the reward for loving (or not loving) the least of one's neighbor, "these shall go away into everlasting punishment: but the righteous into life eternal" (Matt 25:46). Throughout this book I walk a fine line between making love for God/ neighbor a point of salvation; however, it is rather the point that this joint-love commandment should be the normative Christian behavior. Anything less is against God's intended will and plan. Therefore, the Holy Scriptures and God's Holy Spirit are pulling the church back to a commitment to loving both God and neighbor. Anything less is unacceptable!

It is equally important that one understands that fully loving one's neighbor is not possible unless one truly does love the Lord with all one's heart, soul, mind, and strength. Empty and hollow neighborliness only propagates hard feelings and a sense of obligation among neighbors; however, when people are motivated to love their neighbors because of their consuming love of the Savior, community and fellowship are created. True biblical community is driven and defined by the joining in a consuming love of both God and neighbor. It is in such an atmosphere of unity between both commandments that God can work and change lives forever. It is most often (and rightly so) a passionate love for God that motivates missionaries to forsake home, language, and culture to reach the unreached in distant lands, to love new and different neighbors. Home missionaries forsake jobs, security, and personal safety to start churches in unchurched communities among neighbors they have never met. It is the same love for God that should motivate a Christian to shovel a neighbor's walk, help slaughter a hog, share a meal, teach a Bible study, or fellowship with those around them. The best thing a Christian can do for his neighbor is to be consumed by love for his Savior. Love of God and love of neighbor stand together in a dependent relationship. Love for neighbor is not only a love that demands the love for God, but the love for God equally demands the love for neighbor. Each of them is an achievement flowing from the other; it is true that each is the prerequisite condition for the other.

> It is this consuming love for God that will cause Pastor Levi at First Church to reach out and love his neighbors that sit on the pews each Sunday. It is this same love that will motivate him to love those in his community that have never come to church before. It is also the same love Pastor Levi extends to Jim, Sharon, Fred, Sally, and all the rest of his community, through care and fellowship, that will cause them to equally fulfill the command to love the least of their neighbors. This overwhelming love for Christ will cause Jim to reach out and fill Sharon's loneliness and repair their broken marriage. Finally, their newfound love for Christ (and each other) will cause Jim and Sharon to reach out to others they go to church with, those they work with, and the neighbors they are trying to ignore (especially the ones they don't like)!

"Love your enemies, bless them that curse you, do good to them that hate you, and pray for them which despitefully use you, and persecute you" (Matt 5:44). The command to love the least, the worst, and the ones you don't even like is clear in the Scriptures. They warn that, if Christians only love those who love back, they are no different than non-Christians (Matt 5:44–47). Christian love should be extended to both fellow believers (whom they may like) and unbelievers (whom they most often don't like), even when they are hostile and mistreat the Christians. The children of the Father, who seek perfection because he is perfect, love those that are least in this world (Matt 5:48). Jesus was thronged and followed by the least of his world until many criticized even those with whom he ate (Matt 9:10–11). One radical difference between Jesus and other Judaism movements at the time was his concern for the poor, the diseased, the outcast, the strangers, and the marginalized. It does not sound like much with which to start a church, yet Christ chose a ragtag group of sinners (counted the least of their day) to build the biggest and most powerful movement in the world. Two thousand years later, Christ is still asking us, through the second commandment, to love him by loving the least, on whom he is continuing to pour out his Spirit.

The concept of the joint-love commandments is specifically presented in three of the Gospels. In the book of Mark, it is presented as a double commandment where the emphasis seems to be loving "the Lord thy God with all thy heart, and with all thy soul, and with all thy mind, and with all thy strength." However, contextually, the writer of Mark's overall emphasis was that Jesus was the same God the Jews had always worshiped and not about the fulfillment of the two commandments (Mark 12:28–34). In the book of Matthew, the two commandments are considered as equal in importance/emphasis (Matt 22:39–40). The contextual emphasis here is given in consideration of the two commandments as an interpretation of the law, and Jesus demonstrated that, if believers have done both commandments, they have fulfilled the law.

In the book of Luke, the two commandments are fused into one great commandment by a lawyer, who is discussing with Jesus how one might inherit the kingdom of God (Luke 10:25–28). The contextual emphasis here is summed up in the question by the lawyer, "Master, what shall I do to inherit eternal life?" Each of these different references demonstrate the inseparable nature of the two commandments, regardless of the contextual setting; however, it is important to point out that in the context of this book (how the kingdom of God is acquired on earth) the example in Luke is the example of relevance. The two commandments must become one great commandment! "Too often Christians have failed to combine servanthood with truth."[3] Any effort to separate these two commandments is, in essence, "doing violence to what God meant to be joined."[4]

It is equally important to note that the joint concept of loving God and loving neighbor does not start in the New Testament, but rather is part of the very nature of God and is found throughout the Old Testament. The first time the "love thy neighbor" language is utilized is found in Leviticus, "thou shalt love thy neighbor as thyself: I am the Lord" (Lev 19:18). According to Jesus, "On these two commandments hang all the law and the prophets" (Matt 22:40). A brief examination of the Ten Commandments demonstrates that the first four relate to loving God and the last six relate to loving one's neighbor (Exod 20:1–17). Even earlier, God confirmed to Cain that he was his brother's keeper (who happened to be his neighbor) (Gen 4:1–14), and Abraham demonstrated the principle when preferring his nephew Lot's choice of land (Gen 13:8–9) and his concern for the city of Sodom (Gen 14—18).

After the resurrection and ascension of Jesus, the early church lived out the joint-love commandment that he taught them in their day-to-day lives. "As the first family of God under the New Covenant, the early Christians cared for the needs of each other . . . care was extended above all to widows, orphans, the elderly and sick, those incapable of working and the unemployed, prisoners, and exiles."[5] Jesus told his followers, "By this shall all men know that ye are my disciples, if ye have love one to another" (John 13:35). Love for one another and the supplying of one another's needs, "is the key component in a formative Christian environment."[6] Jesus commanded and modeled community, the disciples obeyed his commandment, and Christianity was spread throughout the whole world by the end of the first century. "Love, justice, and compassion were the distinguishing marks of the early church."[7] The second commandment was not an isolated observance but shared throughout the church universally. "Not only was care given by the local congregation to its own members, but care was extended from one congregation to another."[8]

---

3. Sider, *Living Like Jesus*, 169.

4. Homrighausen, *Who is My Neighbor*, 401.

5. Boone, *Community and Worship*, 7.

6. Boone, *Community and Worship*, 7–8.

7. Boone, *Community and Worship*, 6.

8. Boone, *Community and Worship*, 7.

The Neighbor Defined

Throughout the New Testament the word "neighbor" is translated from the Greek word *plesion*. When used as an adverb, *plesion* is translated "near" (John 4:5). When used as a noun, *plesion* is translated "neighbor," meaning one who is close by (Luke 10:27).[9] The commandment to love those who are close by as oneself, and also the commandment to love one's enemies, entirely change the common thoughts on such relationships.

> Your neighbor is not your blood-relation only, not the circle of your acquaintance only, not your countryman or co-religionist only; but he or she whom you can help in any way whatsoever—the wretched tatterdemalion from the slightest contact with whom you shrink; the besotted and degraded; even your enemy, who hates you and despitefully uses you; him, her, mankind, you are to love.[10]

The question, attempting to define one's neighbor, is not a new question but was the same question asked of Jesus before he told the popular story of the Good Samaritan: Who is my neighbor? In answering this question today—in much the same way Jesus did—it's important that we notice the positional references in his answer. When the priest went *"that way*: and *when he saw him*, he passed by on the other side." Next "a Levite, *when he was at the place*, came and *looked on him*, and passed by on the other side." Finally, "a certain Samaritan, as he journeyed, *came where he was*" (emphases added) (Luke 10:29–33). The Good Samaritan found, in the beaten man, a man much like himself: alone, ignored, and rejected by those around him.

Although true biblical neighborliness may go well beyond proximity/location, this is certainly the point Jesus was making in the parable of the Good Samaritan. Even if not limited to proximity, proximity is an excellent place to start loving our neighbors. Sometimes distance (e.g., foreign missions) is a distraction from the neighbor that is within a few feet, and this distraction can become a pacifier that prevents any involvement with those that are closer. It is easier to give fifty dollars to missions each month than to reach out to the neighbor next door. Jesus' only references in this parable are to people that were close by (the neighbor); therefore, "your neighbor is anyone whose need you see, whose need

9. Bromiley, *International Standard Bible Encyclopedia*, 518.
10. Spence, *Pulpit Commentary*, 283.

you are in a position to meet."[11] It is important to couple discipleship training with being a good neighbor while sitting on a pew at church on Sunday morning. After practicing and familiarizing oneself with loving acquaintances and friends, it will become less difficult for the Christian to be a good neighbor to the least of their community.

> *Jim and Sharon could not conceive of reaching out to Sally or the welfare family because they had never experienced neighborly love within the confines of their own church and likely not even their marriage.*

Jesus said it this way, "A new commandment I give unto you, That ye love one another; as I have loved you, that ye also love one another. By this shall all *men* know that ye are my disciples, if ye have love one to another" (John 13:34–35). Christians will be identified by non-Christians as Christians because of their love for others. "We must plead with our broken neighbors like weeping prophets, not denounce them like angry moralists. We must gently throw our arms around all those trapped in sin. Love them into the kingdom, and travel with them no matter what the cost in their journey toward wholeness in Christ."[12]

Jesus, after finishing the parable of the Good Samaritan, spoke to the lawyer and said, "Which now of these three, thinkest thou, was neighbor unto him that fell among the thieves?" (Luke 10:36). Notice that only those that were there weighed into the discussion on who was the neighbor; only the three who had been in proximity (close by) with the wounded man. However, it is important to note that being close by was not enough to fulfill the second commandment. Rather, the lawyer answered and said that it was he on whom the Samaritan showed mercy. Therefore, two identifiable principles are noted when obeying this biblical passage/parable to love one's neighbor: first, one must be there (proximity), and second, one must show mercy.

---

11. Robinson, *Biblical Preaching*, 105.
12. Sider, *Living Like Jesus*, 177.

The Depth of the Neighbor Relationship

Jesus is the true neighbor; neighborliness is part of the incarnate nature of God from the beginning of the world. It would be just as impossible to think of Jesus not being a good neighbor as it would to separate the Father from the Son. "Greater love hath no man than this, that a man lay down his life for his friends" (John 15:13). Surely laying down one's life for another is the total sum of being a good neighbor, and "If any *man* will come after [Jesus], let him deny himself, and take up his cross, and follow [Jesus]" (Matt 16:24). The original sin was not eating the fruit, but it was the determination that Adam and Eve were going to do their own will. From that time until now, sin can be defined as selfishness (nobody, even God, is going to tell me what to do). This self-centeredness is what blinds the church today and keeps it from fulfilling the joint-love commandment. If the church is ever going to deny herself and take up her responsibility (cross) to reach the world, she must join the two great commandments as one great love commandment. The church's responsibility is to do God's will; and it is God's will that the church becomes a better neighbor.

The Second Commandment and the Law

Among most mainstream Christian movements, it has been well established that the church is not under the law, but under grace. The apostle Paul repeatedly stated, "ye are not under the law, but under grace" (Rom 6:14; 10:4; Gal 3:5; Acts 15:5). It is often heard that the law is finished and fulfilled, but rarely does one hear or see a study on how it was, and is, fulfilled. If one were to ask when and/or how this took place, most would simply be told it happened at Calvary. While this is true, it is not a complete enough answer. On Calvary hung the greatest neighbor that ever lived, and Calvary was the greatest act of neighborliness that the world has ever seen. "Greater love hath no man than this, that a man lay down his life for his friends" (John 15:13). Jesus was the perfect model of the second commandment, both before and while on the cross, and our attitude should be the same as his. "Let this mind be in you, which was also in Christ Jesus: Who, being in the form of God, thought it not robbery to be equal with God: But made himself of no reputation, and took upon him the form of a servant" (Phil 2:5–7).

Paul reaffirmed the fulfillment of the law, both from Jesus' demonstration of love on the cross and within Christianity today, by the Christian's love for his neighbor, when he wrote, "For all the law is fulfilled in one word, *even* in this; Thou shalt love thy neighbor as thyself" (Gal 5:14). James, the brother of Jesus and the bishop of Jerusalem, wrote, "If ye fulfill the royal law according to the scripture, Thou shalt love thy neighbor as thyself, ye do well" (Jas 2:8). The law of Moses, although finished at Calvary, written on "tables of stone," was replaced with a new commandment when the Spirit of God wrote, "in fleshy tables of the heart" (2 Cor 3:3). The Spirit of a holy God enables Christians to love their neighbors in the same way they love themselves, thus fulfilling the goal of the law of Moses (Lev 19:18).

The goal of the law of Moses could be split into two major parts. The first part of Moses' law was exemplified in the first commandment Jesus mentioned in the New Testament, "Thou shalt love the Lord thy God with all thy heart, and with all thy soul, and with all thy mind. This is the first and great commandment" (Matt 22:37–38). This first part deals with our relationship with God. Jesus also mentioned the second part of Moses' law in the same passage, "the second *is* like unto it, Thou shalt love thy neighbor as thyself. On these two commandments hang all the law and the prophets" (Matt 22:39–40). The second part of Moses' law dealt with relationship among neighbors, and Moses used the bulk of the laws (rules) to show the children of Israel how to be a good neighbor. However, Paul stated, "all the law is fulfilled in one word, even in this; Thou shalt love thy neighbor as thyself [the second commandment]" (Gal 5:14). This further shows the truth in what was discussed earlier: only when you have loved your neighbor (who could be the least of the kingdom) as yourself, have you loved the Lord with all your heart, soul, and mind.

Paul wrote to the Romans who were finding it difficult to love their neighbors across the racial line between Jews and Gentiles. The Jews wanted the Gentiles to follow the law of Moses, even though no man had ever been justified by the law (Rom 3:20). Paul reminded the Jews and the Gentiles of Rome, in the closing of his book to the Romans, that they did not owe (neither should they require of each other) anything except love (Rom 13:8). Paul then quoted several of the original laws of Moses and summed up the principle behind the law by saying, "if *there be* any other commandment, it is briefly comprehended in this saying, namely, Thou shalt love thy neighbor as thyself. Love worketh no ill to his neighbor: therefore love *is* the fulfilling of the law" (Rom 13:9–10).

In Luke 18:18–22, a certain ruler came to Jesus one day and "asked him, saying, Good Master, what shall I do to inherit eternal life?" Jesus then quizzed him about his adherence to the law of Moses. The young ruler was proud to be able to claim that he had kept all the law from his youth up. However, the man turned away sorrowfully when Jesus said, "Yet lackest thou one thing: sell all that thou hast, and distribute unto the poor, and thou shalt have treasure in heaven: and come, follow me." The man's problem was not that he had money, but rather that he would not distribute his money among the least of his neighbors and therefore demonstrated that he did not love them as he loved himself. The rich men of Jesus' time stepped over and around beggars daily. The rich young ruler could follow the letter of the law, but not the spirit or intent of the law. Many will stand in judgment someday with all of the boxes checked and hear Jesus say, "Yet lackest thou one thing" or, as Jesus warned in the Gospel of Matthew, "Verily I say unto you, Inasmuch as ye did *it* not to one of the least of these, ye did *it* not to me. And these shall go away into everlasting punishment" (Matt 25:45–46).

Lessons Learned: Go, and Do Thou Likewise

Let there be no mistake, the second commandment to love one's neighbor was not, and is not today, a suggestion. Repeatedly, throughout both the New and the Old Testament, loving one's neighbor is referred to as a commandment. The very nature of a commandment is that the injunction is to be obeyed almost without question. Jesus spoke to the lawyer, who stated that both the first and the second commandments were the requirement to obtain the kingdom of God, and said, "Thou hast answered right: this do, and thou shalt live" (Luke 10:28). There is an urgent call to obedience that runs throughout the New Testament for the church to love her neighbors as Christ did . . . "daily, persistently, practically. Jesus modeled servanthood, self-sacrifice, and special concern for the poor and neglected."[13]

Even though the Western Christian world has mirrored the doctrine of individualism and isolation, there is a movement within the body of Christ that is heading back to the joint-love commandments found throughout Scripture. The church must no longer concern themselves with only loving the Lord their God with all their heart, and soul, and mind, but the church must understand that the only way to really and truly love God is to love their neighbors as well. The church must consider

13. Sider, *Living Like Jesus*, 32–34.

her positional relationships and reach out with the love of Christ emanating to those around her. The love of neighbors is not isolated to neighbors within the church but must be extended to even the very least/worst of our enemies. After Jesus identified for the lawyer who his neighbor was, he commanded the lawyer, "Go, and do thou likewise" (Luke 10:37).

> *Pastor Levi, and the church he pastors, must not isolate being the church to three services a week, but must take church beyond the four walls of their building and out into the highways and byways of the community. Pastor Levi must take the church into his own home and into the homes of his parishioners, like Jim and Sharon. When Jim and Sharon see the love for God and neighbor mirrored in the actions of their pastor, Pastor Levi, they will reflect what they see in his example by being the living/breathing/loving church to Sally, the welfare family next door, and even to each other. When this happens, their local church will begin to see the growth that they longed for but had not seen in fifty years. It will all start when someone begins, in response to their love for God, to obey the commandment, "Go and do likewise!" They must go and love their neighbors in the same way they love themselves!*

3

The Second Commandment
and the Church

Beloved, let us love one another: for love is of God; and every one that loveth is born of God, and knoweth God. He that loveth not knoweth not God; for God is love. In this was manifested the love of God toward us, because that God sent his only begotten Son into the world, that we might live through him. Herein is love, not that we loved God, but that he loved us, and sent his Son to be the propitiation for our sins. Beloved, if God so loved us, we ought also to love one another.

—1 JOHN 4:7–11

Unfortunately for Pastor Levi and his local church, the church (at large) has often become a place for singing, preaching, and other things that contribute only towards initial salvation. Because Pastor Levi and the previous pastors neither taught nor demonstrated anything else as the life and actions of the church, the rest of the congregation followed suit. No one saw the church as a place to make friends, create/organize fellowship, share stories, find comfort/ encouragement, and/or find help/assistance in times of trouble. You can be sure that if they did not see their responsibility to those who regularly attended the church, they were certainly not looking to encourage such behavior among their unreached neighbors, the community, and the least of society.

"But be ye doers of the word, and not hearers only, deceiving your own selves. For if any be a hearer of the word, and not a doer, he is like unto a man beholding his natural face in a glass: For he beholdeth himself, and goeth his way, and straightway forgetteth what manner of man he was" (Jas 1:22–24). These pertinent words of James, a servant of God and the author of the book of James, are the driving force behind this chapter on the second commandment and the church. "We must remember that our objectives go beyond the communication of content to the life response of the [church] to the content we teach. We cannot be satisfied that [the church] know the truth. [They] must live the truth."[1] Therefore, loving one's neighbor ministry must go beyond theory, it must be more than an interesting tidbit of theology, it must become a living part of who we are as Christians and the church we attend. Further, one must be concerned with the church's daily practice, not just the theology, of the second commandment: "Thou shalt love thy neighbor as thyself."

This chapter will establish a usable definition (usable by the church) for the term "Second Commandment Ministry" over against other terms such as neighborliness, community, and/or charity. The principle of proximity will be expanded from the Scriptures to undergird the definition with the growing responsibility of the church. Regardless of the shifting cultural and theological landscape, the command to love one's neighbor is timeless and applicable today. The teaching/behavior of Christ and the practice of the early church illuminate/model how the joint-love commandment must be practiced by the church today. The emphasis in this chapter centers around the straight practice (orthopraxis) of the church.

The German theologian Dietrich Bonhoeffer offers this important view and the practice that will be further discussed below, "theology [has] no object for its reflection other than the personal reality of God revealed through concrete human social relations—Jesus Christ existing as community."[2] The inseparable nature of known/studied theology and practiced theology is never more important than in a discussion of the commandments to love God and to love one's neighbor, upon which hang all the law and the prophets. "Theory and practice inform and influence each other in such a way that all practice includes theory, and theory can only be discerned through practice."[3] Therefore, the inability to separate theology

1. Downs, *Teaching*, 34.

2. Anderson, *Shape*, 17.

3. Anderson, *Shape*, 21.

from practice demands that we return to the biblical text to build/develop a definition that outlines the church's role.

A Useable Definition for the Church

One obvious thing in most conversations is the need for defining the basic terms associated with the discussion: e.g., second commandment, community, and neighbor. Some historic authors' definitions are much different than the premise for this research. For example: a common social science definition of community follows, "If we are going to use the word [community] meaningfully we must restrict it to a group of individuals who have learned how to communicate honestly with each other."[4] While some elements of this definition are attractive, this definition is restrictive in nature to a certain group, and a certain learning style, and prohibits the command to go "unto one of the least" (Matt 25:40). Others pointed out that clubs, billiard halls, gangs, schools, colleges, the military, and even prisons are all forms of community. Unfortunately, while all these may be a kind of community, it does not fulfill the breadth of the joint command to love both God and neighbor. Yet others include a love for God and neighbor as they attempt to define community; "Looking to the Lord . . . become embodiments of charity."[5] While this definition is more attractive than the previous, it still seems to fall short of what Christ intended when he commanded the church to "love thy neighbor as thyself."

Therefore, to define the second commandment for the modern church, one must return to the Scriptures to formulate a definition. Consider again the following two passages together: "Jesus said unto him, Thou shalt love the Lord thy God with all thy heart, and with all thy soul, and with all thy mind. This is the first and great commandment. And the second is like unto it, Thou shalt love thy neighbor as thyself. On these two commandments hang all the law and the prophets" (Matt 22:37–40). Also, "Verily I say unto you, Inasmuch as ye have done it unto one of the least of these my brethren, ye have done it unto me" (Matt 25:40).

Throughout this book the second commandment will be understood and defined as: *A commandment that commands the practical demonstration of one's love for his/her neighbor(s), down to the least of them, loving them as one does him/herself and springs forth from the depth of one's love*

4. Peck, *Different Drum*, 59.
5. Swedenborg, *Charity*, 158.

for God. First, it must be remembered that the second commandment is exactly that, a commandment. Therefore, it is not optional, nor a choice, but a commandment that must be obeyed by Christians that love Jesus, "If ye love me, keep my commandments" (John 14:15).

Second, it is the practical demonstration of one's love, rather than an isolated theoretical love. The neighbors of the world need practical love that must extend beyond just praying for them. "What doth it profit, my brethren, though a man say he hath faith, and have not works? can faith save him? If a brother or sister be naked, and destitute of daily food, And one of you say unto them, Depart in peace, be ye warmed and filled; notwithstanding ye give them not those things which are needful to the body; what doth it profit?" (Jas 2:14–16).

Third, Christians who love their neighbors must extend their practical neighborliness down to the very least of their neighbors. Jesus said, "Love your enemies, do good to them which hate you" (Luke 6:27), and James, an early writer for the first church, wrote, "If ye fulfil the royal law according to the scripture, Thou shalt love thy neighbor as thyself, ye do well: But if ye have respect to persons, ye commit sin, and are convinced of the law as transgressors" (Jas 2:8–9). Selective love and neighborliness disregard the intent of the second commandment and the overall mission of the church, both then and now.

Fourth, the practical act of love must be comparable to what one would do for herself in a similar situation. It is important to remember that what is done "unto one of the least of these my brethren, ye have done it unto me" (Matt 25:40). In other words, any act of neighborliness, even down to the least of our contacts, is done as unto Christ himself. From the very earliest writings of Scripture, God has always required the best/first of one's offering; furthermore, God, who knows all things, knows that one treats himself best. Therefore, God wanted his children to do their best for their neighbors and, by extension, do their best for God himself. Finally, when one fulfills the second commandment, as defined, she has also fulfilled the first commandment.

Expanding the Principle of Proximity

There remains an element of the second commandment that many do not address. The whole previous definition eliminates the issue of proximity. When considering proximity, the church must consider again the story of the Good Samaritan as we did in chapter 2: ". . . a certain priest *that way*: and when he saw him, he passed by on the other side. And likewise a Levite, *when he was at the place*, came and looked *on him*, and passed by on the other side. But a certain Samaritan, as he journeyed, *came where he was*: and when he saw him, he had compassion on him" (emphases added), (Luke 10:31–33).

The emphasis here is on the proximity of the participants in the story, and Jesus did not put any responsibility upon anyone who was not within a relative proximity to the man in need of a neighbor. Throughout the New Testament, the word neighbor is translated from the Greek word *plesion*. When used as an adverb (John 4:5), *plesion* is translated "near," and when used as a noun (Luke 10:25–36), is translated neighbor, meaning one who is close by. Therefore, we would add to our definition, *When exposed to others by proximity, the second commandment is a commandment that commands the practical demonstration of one's love for his/her neighbor(s), down to the least of them, loving them as one does him/herself, that springs forth from the depth of one's love for God.* Before we leave the story of the Good Samaritan, it is important to note that Jesus further instructs the hearers of the story and the readers of the Scriptures today, "Go, and do thou likewise" (Luke 10:37). Go and have mercy on your neighbors!

So, two identifiable ingredients are noted in fulfilling the second commandment and, therefore, building biblical community: first, one must be there (proximity), and second, one must show mercy (treat them as one would wish to be treated). The church must shake herself from her comfort and slumber, recognize the commandment to build community, and have mercy on a world that is desperately in need of mercy. "A new commandment I give unto you, That ye love one another; as I have loved you, that ye also love one another. By this shall all *men* know that ye are my disciples, if ye have love one to another" (John 13:34–35).

The Timeless Nature of the Second Commandment

Before the issue of definition, including proximity, can be put to rest, one must consider the evolving nature of time, culture, and age. If nothing else changes, these three elements—time, culture, and age—can be assured to change. However, by defining the second commandment, as has been done above, we have eliminated these three variables from the definition. This does not mean that they do not need to be factored in, because they must be. Throughout this author's efforts to implement the second commandment, I realized the variableness of these elements across the country and its demographics. At first, I tried to provide people with a list of things they could/should do for their neighbors, with very little success. Second, I brainstormed with groups to develop a list and, after it was compiled, I then asked them to choose from the list, and again met with little success.

Finally, I began to teach and preach the timeless biblical principles of the second commandment, while reminding people of their obligation to fulfill the commandment. This allowed them to factor in their own age, culture, and time as they were exposed to various needs; "every congregation is charged with the responsibility of creating community in its own context."[6] It was then that the church and I began to see second commandment ministry in action. One older couple adopted (legally) a middle-aged drug addict and alcoholic, with the intent of long-term rehabilitation. One lady provided clothing and furniture for a family of five, who were also involved in the drug scene and had lost everything they owned for some unknown reason. Two other men started a jail ministry and an outreach to the families of those incarcerated. All these second commandment ministries were more personal for those involved because each one was able to establish the above principle in their personal situation, thus factoring in the variable elements of time, age, and culture.

Personally, I became heavily involved with, and led a team of more than a dozen people to help, a welfare family that was in the process of having their parental rights terminated. The only reason I can state for giving two years and hundreds of personal hours to teaching parental skills, negotiating with state agencies, and a whole lot of elbow grease is that they crossed my path one day just like the Good Samaritan crossed the beaten man's path, and I could not pass them by. While I cannot say that all these outreaches, along with many others, were successful, as men would count success, I can say that each person who was really involved with loving the least of their neighbors would testify of a closer personal relationship with God because of their efforts, and that is what second commandment ministry is all about. While culture, age, and time are factors of great concern for the Western church, "this does not mean that a lively Christian imagination cannot discover many a task of love, communion, and self-fulfillment" through a heartfelt commitment to love one's neighbor.[7]

6. Foster, *Future*, 68.
7. Rahner, *Love of Jesus*, 94.

Defining Community in Context with the Second Commandment

Now that we have a definition for the second commandment, a brief look will be taken at the widely used and variously defined word community. *Community* is a word that, on some levels, seems to defy a definitive definition: "there remains something about it that is inherently mysterious, unfathomable. Thus, there is no adequate one-sentence definition of genuine community."[8] Therefore, community (for the purpose of this book) in context with the second commandment, is better understood as a natural occurrence of relationships that result from loving one's neighbors. Community, such as the community that is generally the result of love between a man and a woman, is difficult to plan for, but seems to be the natural offspring of their love. Community, for the modern church, should likewise be the natural occurrence resulting from loving one's neighbor.

After time, neighbors that work together (the ministers and those ministered to) make their community better. Initially, however, it must be the effortless offspring of selfless love that springs from one's love for God and offered to others without strings attached. This provides the biblical basis for all community associated with the church. Unfortunately, "For some, 'church' is a place or service one goes to on a certain day of the week. Biblically, however, the church is a community or family of people, with Jesus Christ as the head."[9] "The process of community-building begins with a commitment—a commitment of [church] members not to drop out, a commitment to hang in there through thick and thin, through the pain of chaos and emptiness."[10]

This commitment, to loving one's neighbor and participating in practical community, should be the same commitment that brought one to an altar of repentance when she/he first came to the Lord; a commitment to love the Lord with all her/his heart, soul, mind, and strength. Unfortunately, many observers argue that such commitment is not generally found, nor required, by the modern church, and therefore community is stifled at best and non-existent at worst. While the Scriptures insist that community is the natural occurrence of relationships that result from loving one's neighbor, it likely will be secondary to the initial commitment made at Calvary. However, it stands to reason that many modern

8. Peck, *Different Drum*, 59.

9. Anthony, *Introducing Christian Education*, 40.

10. Peck, *Different Drum*, 300.

churches, that are uncommitted to God or neighbor, have little to offer when attempting to love their neighbors, and therefore community is non-existent in many churches.

The First Century Church Practice of the Second Commandment

This will be covered exhaustively in the next chapter but let us summarize for clarity in this conversation. One cannot consider the practice of any theological position without considering how Christ and the early church practiced the same theology. Unless the modern demonstration of the second commandment revolves around the context of the early first century church, then we have only created new theology instead of living the historic commandment to love one's neighbor. Jesus' ministry was noted for its neighborliness to publicans, sinners, lepers, prostitutes, tax collectors, all manner of diseased, the demon possessed, women, Gentiles, Roman soldiers, servants, children, rich, poor, widowed, brokenhearted, captives, and the list could go on indefinitely. Jesus lived the commandment to love the neighbors he encountered, to whom he preached, and demonstrated his ultimate sacrifice for all of his neighbors by ultimately dying for the sins of the entire world (and throughout all history) on Calvary's cross (1 John 2:2).

The early church followed, in both the examples and teachings of Christ, by living and teaching the principles of loving their neighbors. The commandment to "love thy neighbor as thyself" is repeated in Rom 13:9, Gal 5:14, and Jas 2:8, while the concept and the demonstration of love is repeated in every book of the New Testament. Furthermore, the disciples continued in "fellowship, and in breaking of bread" (Acts 2:42), and the apostle Paul entreated the church to "*take upon* [them] the fellowship of the ministering to the saints" (2 Cor 8:4). Also, John said, "But if we walk in the light, as he is in the light, we have fellowship one with another, and the blood of Jesus Christ his son cleanseth us from all sin" (1 John 1:7). "The striking degree of unity and brotherhood within the Christian community is especially manifested by the interest in fellowship, the eating of common meals, and the practice of selling one's possessions in order to share the proceeds with poorer brethren."[11]

11. Niswonger, *New Testament History*, 188.

Interagency Cooperation with Second Commandment Ministry

One fear that is often voiced to promotors of modern second commandment ministry, especially among conservative churches, is the objection to involvement with agencies and/or people who are not of like precious faith. It is assumed that this fear is generated by the thought that somehow these "other" people will change the second commandment minister, or maybe a feeling that they may not be respectful of the minister's beliefs. While this may be true in isolated cases, it is not generally true and is, for the most part, unfounded (in this author's extensive experience, non-existent). "Just because it is important for Christians who differ fundamentally on points of doctrine to keep rigidly separate in matters of worship and religious organization, it is important that they should co-operate on the neutral ground of social work, and on every occasion where no principle is sacrificed by so doing."[12]

Personally, I found the opposite to be true in the parental custody case I mentioned above. When exposed to the need, I had no time to prepare to help this couple. However, I marched into a courtroom to plead with a judge, to intervene in the case and to have the court appoint me as the coordinator of their care, and found a roomful of people that were intimidated by me. I was scared to death, but time after time I stood in that courtroom and felt the power of God sweep through our midst and recognized the court's fear of this aura. The judge remarked that in forty years of sitting on the bench he had never seen a person, or a church, attempt to intervene in such a case, let alone produce the results that he had witnessed over the course of a year. Tears were running down the faces of lawyers, clerks, and family members at the final court hearing, but it was the result of the church working together with many different state agencies. The state had tried for six years to redeem this family, alone they could not do it; however, it is equally true that the church also could not have done it alone (the resources needed were not available without the state's help).

When charity is isolated and uncoordinated, it is generally not effective. As this family's extended community, the church, the state agencies, and the court officials became more familiar with each other and the overall situation. We were quick to realize the truth in the words "it takes a village." As the court-appointed services coordinator for this family, I began to document and unravel dozens of contradictory instructions that had been issued

12. Richmond, *Good Neighbor*, 151–52.

by the uncoordinated efforts of the state. Many times since then, as pastor, I have come to realize that it is my job, as a second commandment minister, to coordinate the available care for the least among us.

I do not go looking for people in need of second commandment ministry; they are sitting on the pews of churches already and cross my path each day. This may include help with their spiritual care, Social Security, disability checks, mental health, healthcare, Medicaid, Medicare, homebuilders, Head Start, transportation, adult education classes, hospitals, clinics, daycare, schools, food pantries, fuel assistance, welfare, college assistance, counselors, battered women's (men's) assistance, SSI, SSD, DYFS, AA, AL-ANON, and more. This sounds like a huge job, and it is, but when a state district judge asks you to stand and explain to the court why you are involved, it is worth the journey. I was able to explain to the court my church's commitment to the first and second commandments, and a room full of professional people will never forget that day. "The world has a right to judge the quality of our discipleship to Christ based on the love we have toward one another."[13]

Pastors and church officials should have a list of local and state agencies, both private and public, that are available in their area. Some pastors have made the excuse that they cannot afford to get involved in second commandment ministry. However, much of the assistance that can be provided for people is available for the asking. Most churches and most people are not aware of the vast assistance that is available for people truly in need. Some communities, such as St. Louis, Missouri, publish a booklet (like the Yellow Pages) that lists the hundreds of assistance agencies and make the booklets available for use by clergy, social workers, chaplains, counselors, and anyone else that might use them. Countless people have sat in my office and cried because they could not pay, for example, their fuel bill (especially in times when fuel costs skyrocketed in the winter). Many were extremely surprised to find out that there were agencies, both private and public, that would assist them in paying for their fuel (if they qualified, and many more qualify than take advantage of it). As a pastor, I could not pay the bill, but as a second commandment minister, I was aware of what was available, and God was able to help them out of a tough spot.

13. Lawson, *Historical Foundations*, 54.

The Value of the Second Commandment

"Let us consider one another to provoke unto love and to good works: Not forsaking the assembling of ourselves together, as the manner of some *is*; but exhorting *one another*: and so much the more, as ye see the day approaching" (Heb 10:24–25). If the church needs reviving and desires to grow, second commandment ministry will provide the incubator for both healing and growth. How can anyone "taste and see that the LORD *is* good" (Ps 34:8) if they never see the church in action? Jesus said, "Ye are the salt of the earth: but if the salt have lost his savour, wherewith shall it be salted? it is thenceforth good for nothing . . . Ye are the light of the world. A city that is set on a hill cannot be hid. Let your light so shine before men, that they may see your good works, and glorify your Father which is in heaven" (Matt 5:13–16). If the world is ever to see the light of the Gospel, they will see the light when the church is being a good neighbor. For too long the church has hidden her candle inside of buildings and within the confines of her own homes. We were not created for isolation and individuality, but rather, we were "created in Christ Jesus unto good works" (Eph 2:10). The world will respond to the light of the Gospel in the same manner one responds to salt. The response is almost automatic; salt is either enjoyed and cherished or spit out and hated.

> Sally, Jim and Sharon's elderly next-door neighbor, while watching their regular trips to church and their perceived happiness, may unfortunately never be close enough to taste the salt of their salvation experience. The lack of fellowship and personal contact prevented Sally from understanding and/or experiencing the love of a sincere neighbor. By extension, Sally did not know the love of the Savior who had died for her salvation. What neither Jim, Sharon, and/or Sally knew is that the God they claim to know puts the solitary in families to alleviate their loneliness (Ps 68:6).

If the church is to see growth and healing, it will be when the church understands that the eye of the world is upon her (as it should be) and provides the world with hope through her actions. "For the earnest expectation of the creature waiteth for the manifestation of the sons of God" (Rom 8:19). The spiritual growth of new converts and the development of relationships with those outside the church are all but impossible unless we encourage one another towards Christian love and being a good neighbor. The church has a responsibility to the evildoers because, by the help of God, the salvation of the evildoers is the "good work" of the church (1 Pet 2:12). The evildoers often glorify God when they see the results of the second commandment in their lives. Furthermore, we must maintain good works because good works (loving one's neighbor) are profitable unto all men (Titus 3:8).

> *Pastor Levi, and his predecessors at First Church, never understood this concept (the necessity of second commandment ministry for healthy spiritual procreation), and consequently spiritual reproduction was a rare occurrence. Furthermore, it never crossed Jim's or Sharon's mind to consider Sally or the welfare family (or even each other) as potential spiritual offspring, and therefore ignored the second commandment to love one's neighbor.*

The most valuable reward connected to the second commandment, which has eternal implications, is the reviving of dried up and/or dying Christians and the birth of new Christians into the body of Christ. David Bernard, a church growth expert, states that 85 percent of all converts come from personal relationships.[14] "The very existence of the church demonstrates [should demonstrate] to the world the truthfulness of the gospel of grace, forgiveness, and reconciliation."[15] It is time for the church to break out of her isolationism into revival with the second commandment. The law of the harvest is "whatsoever a man soweth, that shall he also reap" (Gal 6:7), and the law of judgment is "with what measure ye mete, it shall be measured to you again" (Matt 7:2). These laws bring further value to the second commandment and are illustrated in the life of Dorcas. In the church (in the book of Acts) when Dorcas died, the widows, whom she had loved and to whom she had been a good neighbor, stood by "weeping, and showing the coats and garments which Dorcas made, while she was with them." God heard their weeping, and Peter came from Joppa to pray for Dorcas. After Peter had prayed, he presented her back to her neighbors alive; consequently, many more believed on the Lord Jesus because of her testimony (Acts 9:36–42). In a time when you need prayer, succor, food, or comfort, those that flock to you will be your neighbors,

14. Bernard, *Growing a Church*, 227.
15. Van Gelder, *Essence*, 112.

and their response will be in direct proportion to your previous obedience to the second commandment.

> Not only will obedience to the second commandment reap dividends for the individual Christian, but it will reap rewards within one's circle of influence. Entire churches, like Pastor Levi's First Church, would reap the benefits of a few consumed with a love for God demonstrated to their neighbors. Further, families and extended family members of people like Jim and Sharon, will be saved and blessed because of the example one demonstrates in obedience to the second commandment. Such passion for loving one's neighbor as oneself can be applied to troubled marriages and parenting skills that would give hope for Jim and Sharon's marriage and their children.

In a practical Old Testament example, "Joshua saved Rahab the harlot alive, and her father's household, and all that she had; and she dwelleth in Israel *even* unto this day; because she hid the messengers, which Joshua sent to spy out Jericho" (Josh 6:25). Her willingness to be a neighbor to strangers earned her a spot in the linage of Jesus Christ. In a practical example from the New Testament, one young boy shared his small lunch with five thousand men and their wives and children. Because of this boy's willingness to be a neighbor and share his lunch, a miracle happened, and over five thousand people benefited from this single act of the second commandment (John 6:1–14). For far too long the church experience has been isolated to preaching, singing, praying, and going to church services. It is high time that the whole church becomes part of other important functions of the church as well, such as fellowshipping, discipling, serving, sharing, loving, caring, helping, listening, teaching, and being an example to our communities.

Lessons Learned from the Church Practicing
the Second Commandment

"Ah, this famine of love! How it saddens my soul!" These were words written by Toyohiko Kagawa, a great Japanese Christian, in 1931, shortly before the onset of the Second World War. "Everywhere this dreadful drought of love! Not a drop of love anywhere: the loveless land is dreary. . . When the last drop of love has dried away all men will go mad and begin to massacre all who ever thought of love."[16] This cry for love was a precursor to the Japanese invasion of the world and remains a cry today in a world tormented with war and terrorism. Military might and nationalism fervor has not offered any real solutions to a world that seems about to destroy herself. Now is the time for the true church to arise from the ashes of her complacency and take the helm of second commandment ministries.

The church is daily exposed to the needs of the world around her, and the church is commanded to be a living demonstration of God's love through her to those she encounters on her journey through life. Only when the church loves even the most detestable derelicts of the world's sin-infested societies, in the same way she loves and pampers her own spoiled life, will Christians fulfill the commandment to love God with all their heart, mind, and strength. "The Christian family, salt for society, becomes a vehicle for God to reach out to a misguided, oblivious world that so desperately needs his touch."[17] "But for right now, until that completeness, we have three things to do to lead us toward that consummation: Trust steadily in God, hope unswervingly, love extravagantly. And the best of the three is love" (1 Cor 13:13 MSG).

16. Hutchison, *Christian Love*, 13.
17. Slaughter, *Biblical Perspectives*, 567.

4

The Second Commandment and Early High Christology

And John calling unto him two of his disciples sent them to Jesus, saying, "Art thou he that should come? or look we for another?" . . . Then Jesus answering said unto them, "Go your way, and tell John what things ye have seen and heard; how that the blind see, the lame walk, the lepers are cleansed, the deaf hear, the dead are raised, to the poor the gospel is preached."

—LUKE 7:19–22

The more Pastor Levi of First Church considered the joint-love commandment in the teachings of Jesus and the way in which both he and the early church lived out these revolutionary ideas, the more Pastor Levi realized there was something going on that he had not considered before. What motivated the early church—and Jesus for that matter—to love their neighbors even when their neighbors were often their enemies and sought to kill the believers? Living out these ideas seemed to set the early Christian church apart, from the ordinary Jew, with talk of really loving one's enemies and turning the other cheek. Love the Romans; seriously?

Such ideas about anything but self-love was foreign to their Greek and Roman rulers and even their fellow Jews, who taught that one's obligation extended only to their Jewish neighbors. However, the teachings of Jesus extended Moses' neighborly love of neighbor to include loving Romans, Samaritans, heathens, enemies, and the very least. As Pastor Levi grappled with how to help those struggling in his church, and how little each of them had really done for (loved) their neighbors, he considered what those who first encountered Jesus must have thought about this new teacher. Who was/is he that taught such strange ideas? Some said he was Elijah, Jeremiah, or one of the prophets returned from the grave! One man astounded all when he declared that Jesus was the Christ, Son of the living God (Matt 16:13–16)! Pastor Levi was brought to his knees as he considered the mandate of the first apostles, living out the radical commandment to love all their neighbors in such a time of violence.

CONSIDERING THE MANDATE OF the first-century apostles/church, this chapter will consider what motivated the first church to become followers of this itinerate teacher from Nazareth. However, not just casual followers, but they proceeded to emulate him and teach others around the world to emulate his command to care for the needy, embrace the disenfranchised, and welcome the stranger. This chapter will demonstrate that what the Jewish crowds saw lived out in the hills of Palestine, catapulted early believers into fully embracing Jesus as the Christ, the Son of God. This early Christological acceptance/understanding of the man, Jesus, drove his followers to do great exploits, not just in evangelizing the world, but also in loving the unloved, the enemy, the unseen, the unheard, and the unwanted. This behavior had not been seen prior by the Greek, Roman, and/or even the Jewish cultures that surrounded the first church. Finally, accepting an early Christological understanding by the apostles provided a mandate for the first century church and for those claiming this Christian heritage today.

Early High Christology

The early high Christology debate (when did the apostles fully understand that Jesus was God) has been ongoing, in some form, since shortly after Christ lived upon the earth. Most conservative Evangelicals have argued for an early understanding by Christ's followers. Revelation for the apostles, that Jesus was fully God, began for some of them as early as his baptism and was fully embraced/understood after the resurrection, convincingly witnessed by many. Different scholars have utilized different methods to argue for an early understanding of who Jesus was/is: Howard Marshall's (1934–2015) and Reginald Fuller's (1915–2007) argument was based upon the Christ-hymn in Phil 2:5-11; James Dunn (1939–2020), author of *Christology in the Making: A New Testament Inquiry Into the Origins of the Doctrine of the Incarnation*, spent much of his research on a consideration of the titles of the first century Christ; Larry Hurtado (1942–2019), author of *How on Earth Did Jesus Become God: Historical Questions About the Earliest Devotions to Jesus*, focused on the church's experience of worship and devotion of Jesus as the Christ.

In this chapter, I will not argue for understanding early high Christology from the theology of the Christ Hymn, the titles of Christ, or the devotion/worship utilized by the apostles, but rather from their daily lived behavior. How did they live out the teachings of Christ in the face of unrelenting persecution? Their willingness to counterculturally love (and teach others to love) their neighbors and their enemies is a convincing argument; they did so because they understood Jesus' words and behavior as the words and behavior of the one true God who came to live among men. The followers of Jesus, and ultimately the first church, responded to the acts of Jesus as God, which became the experiences and/or traditions of the church. Just like the acts/behavior of Jesus said something about who his Father was (is), the first church's acts/behavior tell us who they understood Jesus to be.

First Century Culture—Pre-Christian

Before one can fully understand the counterculture posture of Jesus' message and life, it is necessary to place it in the context of his time/world. The first century Roman world was a harsh time, where the downtrodden and disenfranchised were universally scoffed and hated. No one was "friendly toward a man who [had] bad luck, and to the needy, death [was] better than a life oppressed with grievous poverty."[1] While the Greeks had long been defeated, and the Roman world covered most of the civilized world during the time of Christ and the early church, the Greeks still influenced much of the world's culture and philosophy. Along with this combined Greco-Roman worldview there were the cultures and worldviews of hundreds of subcultures, such as Jewish Palestine, that had been conquered by succeeding world powers.

Many Greek philosophers taught followers "to do good to those who love you and do evil to those who hate you," and yet, "pagan society

---

1. Downey, *Who is My Neighbor*, 7.

43

normally made no such provision for the needy."[2] While these ideas existed in the pre-Christian Greco-Roman world, unfortunately, despite such teaching, the Roman Empire could not deal with the large-scale problem of the unfortunate sick and poor in any meaningful way. While Greek society produced skilled physicians and philosophers with lofty concepts of humanitarian service, "the Greek view of man was too deeply ingrained and little was done to provide succor for the needy, the unprotected, and the stranger."[3] In the twenty-first century, while knowledge has increased, not much has really changed. Over 10 percent of the world still lives in extreme poverty (defined as living on less than $1.90 per day).[4]

Unfortunately, a similar charge can be made against the Jewish culture in the first century. The very basis of the law was founded on the Leviticus principle, "Thou shalt not avenge, nor bear any grudge against the children of thy people, but thou shalt love thy neighbour as thyself: I am the LORD" (Lev 19:18). Rabbi Hillel, famous at the beginning of the Common Era, was asked to summarize the law while standing on one foot. His response reflected this principle: "What you hate for yourself, do not do to your neighbor. This is the whole of the law; the rest is commentary. Go and learn."[5]

While this call to love one's neighbor as oneself seems counter-intuitive to my point that unrestricted love of neighbors did not exist, further examination of the writings of Jewish scholars clearly indicates a refusal to accept any responsibility to care for the needy that surrounded them. Rinehart Neudecker states that Hillel, mentioned above, along with Akiva and Ben Azzai, Jewish scholars in the first century, "had only fellow Jews in mind" with no felt responsibility to the stranger. "Apart from the Jew, only the proselyte [was] included in the commandment to love one's neighbor."[6] The refusal to embrace the command to love the stranger as oneself would explain the continual pronouncement of judgment on Israel for their oppression and neglect of the stranger (Ezek 22:7, Jer 22:3).

"Clearly, the love of humankind, universally, is not in view here. In this instance the concept 'neighbor' is restricted to members of one's own group, 'the people of Israel.'"[7] Even later Jewish scholars on the joint-love

2. Downey, *Who is My Neighbor*, 7.

3. Downey, *Who is My Neighbor*, 12–13.

4. Hasell, *Updated International Poverty Line*.

5. Harrington, *Interpreting*, 135.

6. Neudecker, *You Shall Love*, 499, 512.

7. Furnish, *Love of Neighbor*, 327.

commandment wrote, "the commandment to love one's neighbor is to the brother in the Torah and in the commandments," and observed that they were only thinking of Jews faithful to their local synagogue.[8] Lack of responsibility for wronging one's neighbor took an even more unbelievable tone when the "rabbis of the Talmud determined that an Israelite was not [even] liable for murder unless he intentionally killed a fellow Israelite. Indeed, if an Israelite intended to kill a non-Israelite, but killed an Israelite by mistake, he was not guilty of murder."[9]

This seemingly universal refusal to care, by both the Romans and the Jews, for anyone outside their own brotherhood and the continual oppression of those down on their luck was the world into which Jesus was born. Understanding this makes sense of the Christmas story where, even in their hometown, Joseph could find no place for them to spend the night or for Christ's mother, Mary, to give birth. One could argue it was a busy time, but really, Mary was having a baby (but a baby out of wedlock). She was an outcast, unwanted, uncared for, even among her husband's family (Bethlehem was Joseph's hometown), and her perceived indiscretion had made her an other, a stranger, unwanted and unloved. This tells how far the broken world had fallen from where the Father had intended, when even one's family could not see the image of God in the mother of his son.

Christ's Countercultural Presentation

"Master, which is the great commandment in the law? Jesus said unto him, Thou shalt love the Lord thy God with all thy heart, and with all thy soul, and with all thy mind. This is the first and great commandment. And the second is like unto it, Thou shalt love thy neighbor as thyself. On these two commandments hang all the law and the prophets" (Matt 22:36–40). Jesus was born into this narcissistic Greco-Roman world that had oppressed and enslaved the Jewish nation-state of Israel. He began in the earliest moments of his ministry teaching and living out the joint-love commandment to "love God" and to "love one's neighbor as oneself." Following the pattern of the Jewish theology of the time, "Jesus summed up his understanding of [the Jewish] religion as the following of the twofold command . . . to love God and neighbor—but this was nothing new."[10] While this seemed to be

8. Neudecker, *You Shall Love*, 500–501.

9. Hartung, *Love Thy Neighbor*, 4–5.

10. Swidler, *The Jewishness of Jesus*, 106.

parroting the Lev 19:18 principle, it soon became clear that he was teaching something that went much further than anything the world had ever understood or imagined. "Unlike the Jewish rabbinical tradition, [Paul's Epistles and all four Gospels], each essentially independent of the others, all provide evidence that Jesus' use of the joint-love commandment functioned as something more than a summary of the law."[11]

In the third story of the Olivet Discourse, Jesus tells the story of separating the sheep from the goats. "Come, ye blessed of my Father, inherit the kingdom prepared for you from the foundation of the world: For I was an hungered, and ye gave me meat: I was thirsty, and ye gave me drink: I was a stranger, and ye took me in: Naked, and ye clothed me: I was sick, and ye visited me: I was in prison, and ye came unto me." The righteous were astonished and asked the question, When did we do any of these things? We begin to see how Jesus is expanding their understanding when he tells the righteous, "Inasmuch as ye have done *it* unto one of the least of these my brethren, ye have done *it* unto me." The punishment for not fulfilling this expansion of the joint-love commandment to the poor, the stranger, and the lonely is equally as plain, "these shall go away into everlasting punishment" (Matt 25:34–46).

It is equally important that one understands that Jesus was teaching that it is not possible to love the Lord with all the heart, soul, and mind unless one is also willing to love the neighbor and vice-versa. Empty and hollow neighborliness only propagates hard feelings and a sense of obligation among neighbors; however, when people are motivated to love their neighbors because of their consuming love of the Savior, community and fellowship are created. Neighbor-love is driven by the injunction of the joint-love commandment, and neither is possible without the other.

Jesus went even further outside the accepted understanding of brotherhood in Leviticus and included one's enemies, even non-Jews, "Love your enemies, bless them that curse you, do good to them that hate you, and pray for them which despitefully use you, and persecute you" (Matt 5:44). The Scriptures further warn that, if Christians only love those who love back, they are no different than non-Christians (Luke 6:32–36). The children of the Father, his followers, must love those that are least in this world. Jesus' concern for the poor and marginalized was radically different than other Jewish movements. In John's writings, Jesus goes on to identify his followers by this understanding of the two commandments, "By this shall all men

11. Furnish, *Love of Neighbor*, 328–330.

know that ye are my disciples, if ye have love one to another" (John 13:35). This is even more profound when one realizes who his disciples were (publicans, tax collectors, zealots, prostitutes, etc.).

In Luke's parable, the Good Samaritan found, in the beaten man, a man much like himself: alone, ignored, and rejected by those around him. Although true neighborliness may go beyond proximity and need, this is the point that Jesus was making in the parable. Jesus lived and taught this two-fold criterion, proximity and need, for who one's neighbor was in the parable of the Good Samaritan: "Your neighbor is anyone whose need you see, whose need you are in a position to meet."[12] Therefore, once again, Jesus' concept of neighbor extended beyond one's ethnicity and one's social or religious group.

Jesus' perspective on love, neighbor, and justice involved "the transformation of structures and institutions into a moral and ethical design that God intended so that all people could experience wholeness in every aspect of their lives."[13] Jesus proclaimed himself as the bread of life, demonstrating that his concern extended to their physical, societal, emotional, mental, and relational well-being. Jesus identified with the less privileged, thus establishing for all times that any discrimination of any kind was, and is, totally unacceptable. To discriminate in any fashion, even to the least, would be done as unto Jesus. This was no isolated or occasional teaching of Jesus, but the pervasiveness of this in the earliest Christian literature emphasized its importance and suggests that it was characteristic of Jesus' teaching. Completely and wholly loving the least "played a central role in that teaching, and the character of Jesus' whole ministry."[14]

"The biblical idea of justice is comprehensive and practical . . . It is part and parcel of what God is doing in history . . . reconciling humanity to himself."[15] Yet, by the time of the birth of Christ, this mission of practical justice had been replaced by a world of greed that ignored what God desired to do in the world. Therefore, Christ's purpose was to form in the place of Judaism the kingdom of God, and through this new kingdom, instead of Israel, the world would be blessed. There is little question as to this purpose; it was directly quoted by Jesus nine times as "love thy

---

12. Robinson, *Biblical Preaching*, 105.

13. Butrin, *From the Roots*, 84.

14. Furnish, *Love of Neighbor*, 328.

15. Keller, *Generous Justice*, 170.

neighbor;" twice as, "Whatever you wish that men would do to you, do so to them," and once as, "turn the other cheek."

Early High Christology Created Christ-Like Emulation

> Now when John had heard in the prison the works of Christ, he sent two of his disciples, And said unto him, Art thou he that should come, or do we look for another? Jesus answered and said unto them, Go and shew John again those things which ye do hear and see: The blind receive their sight, and the lame walk, the lepers are cleansed, and the deaf hear, the dead are raised up, and the poor have the gospel preached to them. And blessed is he, whosoever shall not be offended in me (Matt 11:2–6).

John's question is the beginning of a transition in the minds of those around Christ, a transition from their understanding of him as merely a good teacher to their recognition of him as the promised Messiah. There are several important items to note in this passage that impact this early high Christological argument. First, this discussion (or inquiry) from the disciples of John was very early in the ministry of Jesus. None would point to this passage (or similar passages) and say that after this the apostles completely understood that Jesus was God. Understanding who Jesus was, was very complicated for them and developed with revelation over the time he was with them. However, if the thought was crossing the minds of the followers of John that early, it was also on Peter's mind when he cried out, "Thou art the Christ, Son of the living God" (Matt 16:16). Further, it was on the centurion's mind at the cross when he observed, "Truly this man was the Son of God" (Mark 15:39). Therefore, it seems impossible to see a later understanding of Jesus as the Christ.

Even more important, the second point to observe in each of these passages is that *they all came to their understanding of who Jesus was because of what they saw him doing.* In other words, he was doing things that they recognized as things that God did (Matt 11:2–6). There is plenty of evidence, as demonstrated above, from a very early point in Christian practice, the underlying root of the apostles' behavior came from their understanding that Jesus was the promised Messiah.

Clearly "the practice of early followers of Jesus, to a large extent, could only be viewed as Christopraxis and that such Christopraxis is based on experience [they had with Jesus]."[16] The actions of the early church could not have been developed from among the Greek philosophers or teachers of the Talmud or the Torah. Therefore, their behavior (praxis) must have been based on the eyewitnesses' accounts of Jesus and the narratives left behind by his followers. We cannot say that God did not intend for the Old Testament Israelites to understand and live out the Lev 19:18 principle in the same manner that Jesus understood and lived out the teachings of the Father. However, we do know that history bears out that during the times of the Israelites it was neither taught nor understood in the same fashion. "While a developing 'high' Christology is frequently associated with liturgical expressions and doxological language, traces of social action in imitation of Jesus' own practice point in a different direction."[17] Therefore, one must conclude that the actions of the Christ-believers were the result of the Christ-actions, and as the son emulated the Father, so the church emulated the son.

The common peasants, among whom the early church found a beginning, was not interested in more empty promises from gods who did nothing or were selective upon whom charity could be imparted. They were interested in this "kingdom of God" movement that could (and did) "do for a lame child, a blind parent, a demented soul screaming its tortured isolation among the graves that mark the village fringes."[18] The pervasiveness of this joint-love commandment is in the earliest Christian literature, and the writers consistently emphasized its importance by their actions. The narratives of the early church indicate that it was not only a characteristic of Jesus' teaching and a characteristic of Jesus' ministry, but a characteristic that made Jesus' ministry recognizable as the work of God.

Almost immediately after Pentecost we see the followers of Jesus emulating his behavior (acting like Jesus). As they had seen the Father through him (John 14:9), the world could now see Jesus through the actions of the disciples (John 13:35). The strong emphasis by the followers of Jesus on the passages with the joint-love commandment, presents a picture that the love of God, demonstrated by Jesus, was one to emulate. "This was one area in which the early Christians [were able to] turn the world upside down."[19]

16. Kazen, *Christology*, 591.
17. Kazen, *Christology*, 591.
18. Crossan, *Life*, 1104.
19. Downey, *Who is My Neighbor*, 15.

"As the first family of God under the New Covenant, the early Christians cared for the needs of each other . . . care was extended above all to widows, orphans, the elderly and sick, those incapable of working and the unemployed, prisoners, and exiles."[20] Jesus told his followers, "By this shall all men know that ye are my disciples, if ye have love one to another" (John 13:35). The church's love for one another and the supplying of one another's needs became the cornerstone of the new Christian church. Jesus modeled community learned from the Father, the disciples modeled community learned from Jesus, and Christianity was spread throughout the known world by the end of the first century. "Love, justice, and compassion were the distinguishing marks of the early church."[21] The martyrdom of many Christians in the first couple of centuries demonstrated how far they would go to emulate the life of Christ.

It is fair to say that other isolated non-Christian groups also cared for the sick as a basic human action of charity and justice, but "when Christians engage[d] in care for the sick, they [did] so in imitation of both the compassion and actions of Christ himself."[22] As the church began to develop beyond its infant stage, it was founded upon these actions of Christ: principles of justice, integration, and restoration; these Christ-actions became the experiences of the Christ-believers. "Many of these practices are associated with Jesus' own example."[23] "These precepts could hardly have been universally practiced, yet . . . members of what he calls the 'peculiar Christian society' practiced them often enough to attract public notice: 'what marks us in the eyes of our enemies is our practice of loving-kindness: 'Only look,' they say, 'look how they love one another!'"[24]

Early High Christological Implications for Today

Jesus was born into a world, both Jewish and Roman, that rejected its responsibility to the needy, the widow, and the stranger. As Jesus lived in his flesh in this world, he emulated his Father to the point that Jesus could say, "he that hath seen me hath seen the Father" (John 14:9)! As Jesus acted in ways that were clearly *like* the Father, the disciples and the first church saw

20. Boone, *Community and Worship*, 7.
21. Boone, *Community and Worship*, 6.
22. Larson-Miller, *Caring for the Sick*, 172.
23. Kazen, *Christology*, 602.
24. Tertullian, *Apologies* 3, 10.

his actions and made the connection that he was the Christ/Messiah. Because the early church saw the actions of Jesus and knew he was the Christ, the converts to Christianity began to emulate the very actions of the Christ and became his body that lived on in the world. Christians today across the world must also emulate the Christ and his historic body if they wish for the world to see Christ in the world today, reconciling the world to himself (2 Cor 5:19). The church must remember what was accomplished by Jesus and the first church, in a world in which the story of the Good Samaritan was a novelty, if they wish to turn today's world upside down.

Jesus was identified as the Christ because of certain characteristics. The disciples and the early church were identified as Christ-followers because of the same characteristics. The challenges/questions for today are: Can the church today also be identified according to those characteristics? Can the church be identified by their actions? Can the church's behavior, that is essential to the church's identity, communicate the transformative power of God to the broken and battered *imago dei*? This transformation requires relationships that are built over time, and it is in these intimate relationships with this "body of Christ" that a new generation of Christ-emulators are born. Just as during the first centuries, the Christian church today must also look for opportunities to be *like* Jesus, and by extension the Father, outside the walls of their church buildings. Fortunately, Jesus' command to love and care for the needy and the stranger was (and is) for all people in all of history. Careful study demonstrates that if the church is to be the church that Jesus intends it to be, such care must be extended to the very least of the kingdom—those that have anguish, pain, hunger, injustice, and death.

This "extraordinary plan and purpose of God" is realized when one is identifiable as the *imago dei* among the "ordinary people who go to work and participate in the local and global economy each day . . . rejoicing that this work touches all facets of life and creates flourishing churches and communities"[25] "As Spirit-filled believers, we have the power and anointing of the Holy Spirit to be his witnesses and to follow the pattern of Jesus in holistic ministry."[26] Such Christian behavior is, in its beginnings, imitative and based upon the stories of Jesus and the early church, but soon becomes one's own attitude and behavior after emulating the life of Christ today and applying it in various contexts.

25. Self, *Flourishing Churches*, 131.

26. Butrin, *From the Roots*, 13.

Lessons Learned from the Behavior of the Early Church

"Change from the way it has always been done to the embracing new paradigms and new ways of thinking entails a process, one that is uncomfortable."[27] This Christological understanding has been challenging the church to think differently and make significant changes for over 2000 years. In every generation such change is uncomfortable as one turns to embrace "the God-ordained mission of the church" in caring for the needy and the stranger.[28] However, "For every victim and perpetrator of the most intimate forms of injustice in our world [yea, to the neediest or the most different], there is hope, forgiveness, and a future of freedom to be found in Jesus, our Redeemer, Healer, and Lord."[29]

In this chapter we have examined the culture of the Jewish and Roman societies and how that, for the most part, the world in question ignored the needy and, at a minimum, shunned the stranger. Into this world was born a man named Jesus who preached a strange and beautiful message of hope to the world's disenfranchised masses. He was soon identified as the Christ, the Messiah, the one foretold by the Old Testament prophets who would set at right the kingdom of God in the world. The disciples and the first church identified this man Jesus as one who came "in *the form* of God" and yet served the world as a "servant." Therefore "God also hath highly exalted him, and given him a name which is above every name: That at the name of Jesus every knee should bow, of things in heaven, and things in earth, and things under the earth; And that every tongue should confess that Jesus Christ is Lord, to the glory of God the Father" (Phil 2:5–11).

The early church emulated this Christ and took on the very characteristics of him during their ministry on earth among the very least and among the strangers. Because of such emulations, the early believers were called Christians (like Christ) and the church existed in the world as the body of Christ that remained in the world to reconcile it to the Father and be a blessing among the nations. Finally, the church today must understand, if the world is to recognize the church as Christ's body today, the church will have to emulate the characteristics of the Christ among the very least, the very poor, and the stranger. It is when humanity sees the church being the church, a church that, like the Christ, has

27. Butrin, *From the Roots*, 171.

28. Corbett and Fikkert, *When Helping Hurts*, 15.

29. Wacker, *Heaven Below*, 159.

God-like characteristics, they will accept the Christ for themselves and glorify his Father which is in heaven. "Human beings will only be drawn out of themselves into unselfish acts of service to others when they see God as supremely beautiful,"[30] and they will only see God as "supremely beautiful" through a church that has emulated his son.

"He hath shewed thee, O man, what is good; and what doth the Lord require of thee, but to do justly, and to love mercy, and to walk humbly with thy God?" (Mic 6:8). This ancient text is a summary of the Bible's message on how to live—we must do justice, act out of merciful love, and walk humbly with God. The concluding point of this chapter is a compelling command to obey and can be summed up in the words Jesus spoke to the disciples after washing their feet, "For I have given you an example, that ye should do as I have done to you" (John 13:15).

> *Pastor Levi found himself weeping in an altar of repentance. How many times had he visited the nice homes of his parishioners and avoided the poor and needy nearby? How many injustices had he ignored because it was inconvenient, uncomfortable, and honestly sometimes downright embarrassing? How many times did he visit Jim and Sharon's home and ignored the unkept homes nearby? He had even listened to their complaints about the "old" lady and the welfare people, not realizing that God had placed Jim and Sharon there to let the light of Christ-like behavior shine hope. He had little time for the unprofitable and seedy elements of his town. Pastor Levi realized that this was God's church and God's town. As he wept in repentance, he realized that in his negligence of Jim and Sharon's neighbors, he had lost Jim and Sharon as well! Maybe if they had seen their pastor's example of love poured out for their neighbors, they would have shared that neighbor love with each other. Further, if Jim and Sharon had not been so isolated and had been Christ-like to their neighbors, their marriage would not have fallen apart.*

30. Keller, *Generous Justice*, 182.

5

The Second Commandment and Modern Pentecostal Movements

Ye shall receive the gift of the Holy Ghost. For the promise is unto you, and to your children, and to all that are afar off, even as many as the Lord our God shall call . . . And they continued stedfastly in the apostles' doctrine and fellowship, and in breaking of bread, and in prayers.

—ACTS 2:38–42

After several days of studying the second commandment and the implications for his church and ministry, Pastor Levi began to speculate on two things: first, he wondered about the impact (or lack) of the second commandment upon the Christian/Pentecostal movement over the last 125 years (both in America and abroad). Second, he was puzzled that he had never heard any preaching, attended any conferences, or even took any classes in Bible school that emphasized the importance of loving one's neighbor. Could revival (or lack of revival) be linked to one's emulation of the behavior of Christ and the early church? Heading to the library, Pastor Levi wondered what recent historic evidence existed.

PENTECOSTALISM EXPLODED IN THE twentieth century, a movement unlike anything anybody had seen for almost two thousand years. It leaped to center stage with five hundred million adherents by the end of the twentieth century. It is stated that it started with one woman, Agnes Ozman, who on January 1, 1901, received her personal Pentecost. Pentecostalism succeeded in defying all odds, all opposition, all criticism, and all persecution, to become the fastest-growing religious movement of all times. Pentecostalism arrived in many forms: classical Pentecostals, Charismatics, neo-Pentecostals, third wavers, and renewal Christianity. However else they may be different, they share three major tenets of faith: glossolalia (speaking in tongues—another language), premillennialism (the expectation of Christ's return), and divine healing.[1] It is upon these three issues that the expanding world of Pentecostalism turns.

This growth has caught the attention of the church world, and they have begun to ask the much-needed question: Why? This chapter will specifically examine the role the second commandment played in the Pentecostal explosion of the twentieth century, with a brief look at the Pentecostal community perspective; examine what role, if any, the second commandment played in the first decade of modern Pentecostal movements; compare Pentecostal acceptance in the twentieth century between North and South America; and learn some lessons from the information presented.

A Pentecostal Perspective of Community

Despite their unity on issues like premillennialism and glossolalia, there often seems to be little else upon which Pentecostals agree. For example, the Pentecostal perspectives on the church are many. The question of authority in the church became important in the new movement, and modern Pentecostals were born to resist against any authority but the Holy Spirit. Consequently, the Pentecostal experience did not yield a single ecclesiological teaching, but a wide variety of traditional forms of church government can be found among Pentecostals. The lack of a universal idea of church prevented a common perspective on what the church should look like and whether the church was only praying, singing, and preaching. Could the church also include feeding the hungry, clothing the naked, and loving one's neighbor? In early modern Pentecostal movements, both doctrine and practice were "often minimized and taken for granted"[2] and left, for the most part, to individual interpretation.

---

1. Dayton, *Theological Roots*, 15–28.
2. Horton, *Systematic Theology*, 22–23.

North American Pentecostals normally think in terms of individuals and the individual infilling of the Holy Ghost. It was only later that Pentecostals acknowledged the possibility that whole communities could also be impacted, and therefore outward behavior might affect acceptance of the Pentecostal message. In the first decade of the twentieth century, the Pentecostal church was prone to only consider the spiritual well-being (salvation) of the individual. If the early movement did not recognize the foundational significance of loving one's neighbor, then part of their understanding of what the church should be was tarnished. In other words, for pastors to take corrective action, they must consider the individualistic nature of North American Pentecostal roots. By recognizing the biblical path from which they (and/or their ancestors) deviated, they can find the path to second commandment ministry and church renewal. If this analysis is correct, one would do well to engender serious theological reflection on the relationship between ecclesiology (study of the church) and soteriology (study of salvation). A more authentic understanding of the impact that comes from loving one's neighbors will enhance the relationship of the Spirit with the church and their ultimate salvation. In other words, Christians must take another look at how they *do* church and what it constitutes to *be* the church.

Community in the First Decade of
Modern Pentecostal Movements

Unfortunately, "The . . . extensive documentation for saints' mundane social lives simply is not available."[3] Herein lies a major obstacle to this historic research, and therefore must be done with an abundance of circumstantial evidence. There is no shortage of legitimate records of the vast volume of classical Pentecostal church services. "Meetings followed daily and nightly . . . Prayer was held day and night . . . No one would be likely to complain about all night meetings . . . That meeting lasted for over three years, going on day and night without a break."[4] "The services ran almost continuously. Seeking souls could be found under the power almost any hour, night, and day."[5] "[S]he personally conducted twenty-one

---

3. Wacker, *Heaven Below*, 197.

4. Ewart, *Phenomenon of Pentecost*, 1–62, 77.

5. French, *Our God is One*, 47.

services per week for the faithful."[6] What little one can surmise from diaries, letters, and autobiographies is that Pentecostals attended church six or more times each week, and, at least partly, it was because it offered a time of rewarding fellowship. While the focus was upon individual salvation, it did not preclude the services from having the added (unforeseeable to some) benefit of community, even though initially fellowship was discretely denied in regular worship meetings.

It is worth noting that Grant Wacker claimed, "The [Pentecostal] revival never had much of a social program."[7] This will be especially important when we see the different perception of Pentecostalism in South America below. "Jeffery Gros, a Roman Catholic ecumenist . . . commented that 'Pentecostals [in Latin America] don't have social programs, they are a social program.'"[8] This difference, as I will explain below, gives rationale to the repeated explosion and fizzle of revival throughout the first two decades of Pentecostalism in North America and the general rejection of it by much of the North American population. Wherever Parham went, he left behind people who believed that they had been transformed by a powerful encounter with the living Christ. Unfortunately, he rarely left them with any sense of community or continuity in the form of a church or fellowship group. "Despite [Parham's] heartening beginning, committed supporters were few, and within several months Parham's ministry [once again] had disintegrated."[9]

This is not to say there was no community at all. For wherever there are humans, they will seek out community with other like-minded folks. Officially, however, fellowship and community were worldly and unnecessary. Part of this was due to the belief in the imminent return of Jesus Christ for the church. Wacker (mentioned above) argued that while there did not seem to be much fellowship outside of church services, it can be found if one looks behind the verbiage of the time. For example, while playing baseball was a sin, building faith/healing and missionary resting homes were in. Wacker theorized that a week at a faith home replaced the recreation and fellowship once enjoyed during a week at the beach. A day spent at

6. Synan, *Century*, 135, 251.

7. Wacker, *Heaven Below*, 136.

8. Synan, *Century*, 135, 294.

9. Blumhofer, *Restoring the Faith*, 43.

camp meetings in "earnest devotion to God" was often spent enjoying and consuming "baskets containing the fat of the land."[10]

Few ever stopped to think about the effect the stifling of community had upon second commandment ministry and, consequently, on the early Pentecostal movement around the country. Kurt Berends, with the benefit of one hundred years of hindsight, offers the following example of the effect of community involvement and acceptance. He researched two churches and the towns in which they were built (Canaan and Jefferson, New Hampshire) by the Harvester Pentecostal movement (found only in the northeastern part of the United States). Berends' opening point in this dialogue is, "Several factors other than tongues speaking proved to be significant in determining what type of reception the Harvesters received."[11]

Both churches were founded in rural New Hampshire farming towns in the year 1907. There was little difference that could be noted other than Jefferson seemed to have more established churches and secret societies than Canaan did. What can be established is that a different approach was utilized by the founders. In Canaan the first family to be converted, who would become the backbone of the church, was George Barney and his family. He and his family had been long-time residents in the area, active in all aspects of community life, and their name was well established in the countryside. The immediate and extended family of George Barney was active in the local economy and government. In 1956 the beautiful brick uptown church, founded by Barney, joined the Assemblies of God and changed its name to the Canaan Assembly of God, as it remains to this day. "Instead of criticizing the [Pentecostal Church], the paper [Canaan Reporter] praised it, noting, 'The work . . . is progressing rapidly towards completion . . . for this little church which means so much for this society'"[12]

Not far away in Jefferson, another church was also founded by the Harvesters and was pastored by a man named Wright. "Throughout much of his ministry Wright [Jefferson's founding (and only) pastor] exhibited a proclivity for confrontation." The *Jefferson Times* and the *Jefferson Democrat* both noted the violent attacks Wright made on the establishment (denominational religion and other town societies). Furthermore, and probably because of his violent attacks, Wright was unable to attract prominent community members into his fold. Less than one year after its

10. Wacker, *Heaven Below*, 134.

11. Berends, *Social Variables*, 72.

12. Berends, *Social Variables*, 72–77.

humble beginning, around 1 a.m. on December 8, 1908, someone threw several sticks of dynamite through the newly-built church window and blew the church level with the ground. That was the end of Pentecostalism in Jefferson, New Hampshire.[13]

One of the fundamental differences between Canaan and Jefferson was the Barney family. "Their social respectability and community involvement offered credibility to the fledging Pentecostal movement in Canaan." While in fact many did disagree with the Pentecostalism of the Barney's, they accepted Pentecostalism because the Barneys were "hard-working contributors to the welfare of the community."[14] "Their [the Barneys] involvement, more than anything or anyone else, proved to be the decisive variable in the region's open-armed welcome to the Harvesters and their message . . . their role in the daily life of the community led to the region's open-armed welcome to the Harvesters."[15] It is important to note that it was not speaking in tongues that caused the rejection of Pentecostalism in Jefferson, but rather the constant attacks led by Wright were both annoying and offensive to the people they wanted to win.

Pentecost Finds Acceptance in North America

"Since the Pentecostals so completely rejected society, it is not surprising that society rejected the Pentecostals. This period of rejection lasted roughly from 1906 to 1923, when Aimee Semple McPherson with her Foursquare Gospel movement gave Pentecostalism its . . . first taste of acceptance by the public."[16] Although much negative has been said about McPherson, her vision, of what the church should be, set the pace for the next twenty years. With a price tag of 1.5 million dollars (dollar value for 1923), McPherson built the Angelus Temple in Los Angeles in 1923 that sat 5,300 people. For twenty years the temple was filled to capacity every time service was held, with thousands being turned away at the door. "In the beginning, she personally conducted twenty-one services per week for the faithful . . . popular demand quickly overwhelmed her. People stood in line for hours for seats."[17]

13. Berends, *Social Variables*, 81–85.

14. Berends, *Social Variables*, 83.

15. Berends, *Social Variables*, 72–77.

16. Synan, *Century*, 190–91.

17. Synan, *Century*, 135, 251.

McPherson's talent was the ability to present the Gospel in a package that both individuals and communities could accept. Her key was showing her followers how to love God by loving others. Her most impressive achievement in the 1930s was a social program where she fed and clothed the poor (forty thousand meals per month). "When the great Depression hit the nation after 1929, the temple fed and clothed more than 1.5 million needy people in the LA area. Because of her love for the poor, Sister Aimee won the everlasting love and devotion of the down-and-outers."[18] The Angelus Temple was known because of their goodwill programs that fed the hungry during the Depression and responded to natural disasters in the California area. McPherson found that the public would be more receptive to the message they desired to deliver if they used a sense of community involvement within which to present and live the gospel. "The advent of Aimee Semple McPherson marked a turning point in the history of the Pentecostal movement in the United States . . . she did much to add interest and toleration to a religion that had been considered of interest only to the lowest levels of society."[19]

When one considers the eulogies of other Pentecostal successful pioneers, this common theme of loving one's neighbor is easily discernable: "if there was a need, [Albert Abbey] helped . . . [Harry] Branding was always very thoughtful and respectful of the elderly . . . [William H. Ring] liked visiting the hospital and won many friends during his lifetime . . . [J. W. Wallace] always [was] a doer."[20] "[Winfred Black] loved people and people sensed that love, for it was not just demonstrated from the pulpit, but was part of his everyday life . . . [Arnold H. Browning] had always been active in working and doing things with his hands . . . on Indian Mission projects . . . [Roy D. Gibson] is affectionately referred to as 'Popsy', and is loved by the young as well as the elderly . . . [W. M. Greer was] kind, considerate and gentle with those who needed help . . . through [M. J. Wolf's] love, I realized what the love of God must be like."[21] Over the last one hundred years, Pentecostalism has found success, not because it has rejected the basic tenets of orthodoxy, but rather because it has coupled truth with community.

18. Synan, *Century*, 135, 251.

19. Synan, *Holiness-Pentecostal*, 200.

20. Wallace, *Profiles, Vol. I*, 18, 36, 194, 268.

21. Wallace, *Profiles, Vol. II*, 41–42, 76, 91–92, 177, 265, 396.

Pentecost Finds Acceptance in South America

If the growth of Pentecostalism has been great in North America, "The growth of Pentecostalism among Spanish and Portuguese-speaking people of North and South America has been phenomenal."[22] Pentecostal evangelism among Spanish-speaking people groups "have been the most successful ethnic-directed efforts . . . pursued."[23] There is little doubt that this success is attributed to the social aspect of Pentecostalism in South American cultures. "Jeffery Gros, a Roman Catholic ecumenist . . . commented that 'Pentecostals don't have social programs, they are a social program.'"[24] As was contrasted earlier, consider this up against what Grant Wacker claims about early Pentecostal movements in the United States: "The [early Pentecostal] revival never had much of a social program."[25] It should be no surprise, that while the outpouring of the Pentecostal message originated in North America, in seventy-five years it was surpassed by the Pentecostal movement in South America.

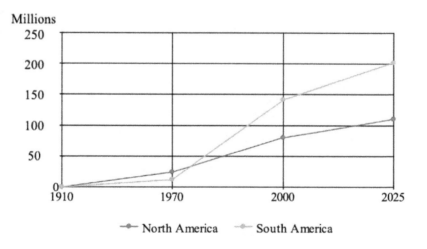

Modern Pentecostalism Growth and Projection

It has been argued that Pentecostalism is more adaptable to the Latin culture. "Much has been written about the Latin American character,

22. Synan, *Century*, 293.
23. Blumhofer, *Restoring the Faith*, 244.
24. Synan, *Century*, 294.
25. Wacker, *Heaven Below*, 136.

whose traits include innate warmth and hospitality."[26] However, this is no defense to those that lack this second commandment nature, the very nature of Christ. "Greater love hath no man than this, that a man lay down his life for his friends" (John 15:13). Latin American Pentecostal pastors, although they may have been influenced by the liberation theology, were still following the example of Christ. Latin American pastors serve as more than just spiritual advisors; they often act as public representatives of the unemployed and dispossessed. South American Pentecostalism serves "as a protective social capsule that renews the broken ties of family, community, and religion in an atmosphere of hope and anticipation."[27]

Gamaliel L. Morales, a Pentecostal missionary to Venezuela, explained Pentecost's success in South America in the *International Review of Missions* with the following story. G. F. Bender arrived in Venezuela on February 25, 1914, and founded an independent Pentecostal movement there. While he was only the first of many to preach the Pentecostal message, he is considered both the father and the most successful proponent of the Pentecostal message in Venezuela. Morales attributes this to "his concern for orphans and the needy . . . his desire to help with primary education for those who had no opportunity to go to secular schools."[28]

In Latin America, Pentecostals are "responding to the vital needs of marginalized populations."[29] "Hunger, misery, marginalization, poverty, injustice, repression, loneliness, and exploitation typically describe the situation prevailing among the impoverished masses of Latin America."[30] Instead of being overwhelmed, missionaries have looked on the field that is white unto harvest, rolled up their sleeves, got down in the dirt beside the downtrodden, picked up their burdens, and took them to Jesus. "In the practice of [South American] Pentecostalism, the neglected sectors and the poorest members of the population find a type of participation denied them by the dominant society . . . the Pentecostal movement in Latin America . . . has shown a concern for such people."[31] Therefore, Pentecostals will continue to grow in numbers and influence in Latin

26. Synan, *Century*, 315.

27. Synan, *Century*, 316, 293–294.

28. Morales, *Moving Forward*, 505.

29. Bastian, *New Religious Map*, 335.

30. Morales, *Moving Forward*, 510.

31. Morales, *Moving Forward*, 511.

America, because they have proven themselves capable of responding to the immediate concerns of their neighbors.[32]

Community and Church Growth

For a long time, researchers of church growth were willing to denounce Pentecostalism; however, due to the phenomenal growth in Latin America (and other areas), they have begun serious consideration of the cause and social effect of this unexpected change. "Had the Pentecostals been just another isolated sect emphasizing controversial doctrines . . . their existence could have probably been ignored. The inconvenient reality of Pentecostalism was its pervasive expansion and presence around the world."[33] Five hundred million (plus) Pentecostals, 1/12 of the earth's population, has turned the heads of the scoffers and doubters. While Pentecostals must never forget the truths poured out in the early days of the last century, it is important to understand that growth has come, in part, to those that have learned, either biblically or culturally, the importance of the second commandment.

"The God of the Bible is a God who loves the poor. It is true that he loves all people, including the rich; but, if we take the Bible seriously, we know that he has a special bias for the poor . . . God raised up the Holiness/Pentecostal movement to minister to the poor once again . . . Check it out . . . This is one of the strongest characteristics of Pentecostal growth."[34] Remember the words Jesus cried out in the synagogue that day, "The Spirit of the Lord is upon me, because he hath anointed me to preach the gospel to the poor; he hath sent me to heal the brokenhearted, to preach deliverance to the captives, and recovering of sight to the blind, to set at liberty them that are bruised" (Luke 4:18).

Lessons Learned From Early Pentecostal Movements

If one were to synthesize all the lessons that could be learned from this historic research on the cause(s) of the massive Pentecostal growth in the twentieth century, they would be capsulated in the first and second

32. Synan, *Century*, 322.

33. McClung, *Azusa Street*, 110.

34. McClung, *Azusa Street*, 129.

commandments. "Jesus said unto him, Thou shalt love the Lord thy God with all thy heart, and with all thy soul, and with all thy mind. This is the first and great commandment. And the second is like unto it, Thou shalt love thy neighbor as thyself. On these two commandments hang all the law and the prophets" (Matt 22:37–40). God's true church must equip itself with gifts and ministries that will fulfill the redemption of all people everywhere, focusing especially upon those who are enslaved by sin, victims of acts of violence, and those who live in degrading and unjust systems. Churches often fail to provide second commandment ministry and, consequently, they have stagnated and not grown, while other churches, that started in a park or storefront twenty years ago, have exploded to thousands of members while providing second commandment ministry to its community. Although most would argue that church growth couldn't be solely the result of second commandment ministry, it is a major contributing factor.

Pentecostal churches "are generally made up of women, peasants, blacks, indigenous people, young people, workers, students, taxi drivers, etc. We are calling on the vital forces in . . . Pentecostalism to take up with renewed urgency the historic role we must fulfill for the church."[35] It is there among the poor, the downtrodden, the sinners, and the common people that the Pentecostal church, with its emphasis upon God's Spirit, is needed. Pentecostalism's spirituality should, by being involved in second commandment ministry, convey to everyone in the community, "this is the way that we live" and should "challenge all persons to be morally responsible for both the way they live in community and for the ways by which they influence the lives of others."[36] The mission of the church must be to build into the daily lives of humanity that loving one's neighbor is according to God's will in both the community of faith (the church) and the world (everything outside the church). The world must not only hear (preaching) of God's love but must also see God's love in the lives of Pentecostals today.

The Pentecostal explosion will, by most expectations, march on through the twenty-first century. If so, at the present growth of Pentecostalism, 1/6 to 1/3 of our earth's population will be claiming a Pentecostal experience by the year 2100. The amount of growth will be determined by how closely we embrace the principles outlined in the first and second commandments. What South America demonstrated culturally is possible and must be endorsed biblically throughout the world. North America

35. Morales, *Moving Forward*, 511.
36. Boone, *Community and Worship*, 4–5.

has attempted to demonstrate and preserve her individuality, even within the ranks of the church. This individuality has cost her the revival that South America, Africa, and China have enjoyed. This trajectory must be corrected, unless one wants to miss the goal intended by Christ. The story of the Good Samaritan is calling to North American Pentecostalism across two thousand years of proven validity; the social-spiritual matrix of the church must be "permeated by the ideals, values and ethics of the kingdom of God . . . [e.g.] love, justice, and compassion."[37]

> *Pastor Levi was shocked at the difference in the growth of Pentecostalism in North and South America. While North American Pentecostalism had good growth, they also had all the money, all the education, and all the talent. Yet, South American Pentecostalism had grown double that of North America. Pastor Levi recognized that while they had preached the gospel of the apostles, no one would recognize them as a Christian from their behavior. This North American individualism had created a scarcity of second commandment ministry that kept Sally and the welfare family from hearing the salvific preaching of Pastor Levi and from being attracted to First Church. Individuality and a lack of teaching about the command to love one's neighbors had prevented Jim and Sharon from reaching out to love and help their neighbors. It also had enhanced Jim and Sharon's individuality within their own home. While they lived together, they had separate lives without real community, without communication, and without dependency. If they didn't understand the command to love the neighbor they shared a home with, there was no chance they would understand the command to love their neighbor next door. Unfortunately, their marriage was dying, their church was shrinking, and sadly, the neighbors were still lost, lonely, and unreached.*

37. Boone, *Community and Worship*, 4–5.

—— SECTION TWO ——

Practicing the Second Commandment (chapters 6–10)

> Lord, when saw we thee an hungered, and fed thee? or thirsty, and gave thee drink? When saw we thee a stranger, and took thee in? or naked, and clothed thee? Or when saw we thee sick, or in prison, and came unto thee? And the King shall answer and say unto them, "Verily I say unto you, Inasmuch as ye have done it unto one of the least of these my brethren, ye have done it unto me."

—MATT 25:44–46

What does the Bible teach us about living the Second Commandment?

UP TO THIS POINT, consideration has been given to the second commandment found in Matthew chapter 25, largely from both the biblical and theological practices of second commandment ministry. From this point on (in chapters 6–10), this book will look at specific practical applications of the second commandment theology outlined in chapters 2–5. In chapter 6, the second commandment will be presented as the foundation of pastoral care provided to the church; in chapter 7, readers will learn that loving one's neighbor is the core motivation of Christian education;

in chapter 8, love that envelopes one's neighbor opens closed doors to pastoral counseling; in chapter 9, love of neighbor is the desired care at the time of death; and in chapter 10, the second commandment becomes the gospel extended across cultures, ethnicities, geographies, skin color, language differences, gender variances, age barriers, and so much more. The reader may jump to the parts that are of personal interest or needed in the moment. However, this author recommends, to fully understand the expansive and exhaustive nature of Christ's command to love one's neighbor, all this section should be read.

Section Two—The second commandment in . . .

- Chapter 6—Pastoral Care
- Chapter 7—Christian Education
- Chapter 8—Christian Counseling
- Chapter 9—Ministering at the Time of Death
- Chapter 10—Intercultural Settings

6

The Second Commandment
in Pastoral Care

That there should be no schism in the body; but that the members should have the same care one for another. And whether one member suffer, all the members suffer with it; or one member be honoured, all the members rejoice with it.

—1 COR 12:25–26

Pastor Levi had always been the kind of pastor that pastored from the pulpit. If he saw needs, problems, and/or sins in the congregation, he would work them into his sermon. Hopefully he would present it in a way that the sermon did not make it apparent that he was addressing an individual. Most of the time it worked, but occasionally it was a disaster, and a few times people had quit the church because of his method. Now it would be easy to be critical of Pastor Levi, but in total transparency, that is the way his pastor had done it. Further, he had no formal pastoral schooling/ training and had learned on the job (sometimes by trial and error). As well, Pastor Levi had been advised not to fellowship with the saints, and therefore he really didn't know them well. Finally, he felt uncomfortable, due to his lack of formal training, in getting too involved with pastoral counseling, advising, assisting, comforting, correcting, and/or caring for the individual.

None of the preachers he knew over the last fifty years did any of that. He remembers well, when he was younger, preacher friends belittling preachers who got involved in all that modern

> *psychobabble. But now, as Jim and Sharon's marriage fell apart, "old" Fred lay dying, several immigrants kept coming to church, and no one knew how to reach out to Sally or the poor/broken in their town, Pastor Levi knew something needed to change. Especially if the church was going to grow, and the broken were going to find help and welcome at the foot of the cross.*

IN THIS CHAPTER, WE will consider the relationship between the second commandment (loving one's neighbor) and the subject of pastoral care (biblically, theologically, practically). We will consider what pastoral care means and how involved pastors, church leadership, and/or church members should become in caring for others. Who should be involved in providing pastoral care to the church and the community, or is this only something the pastor should do? Can the church/pastor provide care to the congregation/community without formal training, and if so, what should one do if the care needed is beyond one's ability (training, skill, finances, space, etc.)? Finally, we will consider working together with other agencies, referring care out to other caregivers, and how to find resources.

What is Pastoral Care?

Quite simply, pastoral care is the art and act of caring for the body of Christ, and the church is that body (1 Cor 12:27)—caring for both those who are already the body of Christ and those who will potentially become the body of Christ in the future. It is not the point of this chapter/book to educate one completely on pastoral care; however, a basic understanding is needed to fully understand how foundational the second commandment is to pastoral care. Also, by extension, just as loving one's neighbor is a commandment, pastoral care is the natural outcome of such a commandment. Thus, caring for the body of Christ is part of what the church is called to do. There are many methods that can be utilized based upon the caregiver's training, but a narrative method (*see Pastoral Care Diagram*[1] *below*) focuses on the stories/experiences of God, the care seeker, and the caregiver. This simple methodology works well in our postmodern world (that focuses upon experience and stories), the literary method of the Scriptures (the Bible is God's story), and fits well with a high view of the

---

1. Peyton, *Modern Exodus*, 2022.

Scriptures (the biblical story is the Word of God for today). A narrative method focuses on how the stories of the care receiver and the caregiver can together become part of the ongoing story of God. In this explanation/chapter, this author will focus upon this method.

Pastoral care is understood best by approaching the subject from three perspectives (*see Pastoral Care Diagram below*). First, and maybe the most important of these points, is *assessing* the care needed by listening to the care seeker's stories and/or experiences. Just as a medical doctor must fully assess the needs of one sick and/or injured, pastoral caregivers must also assess the needs of the individual and/or body of Christ. Second, pastoral caregivers must consider the full range of possible *outcomes/goals* that God desires for his body. From healing to liberation, God desires to meet and care for all our needs according to his riches in glory (Phil 4:19). Third, pastoral caregivers must care for a full range of what it means to be wholly human (the *facets* of care). To consider only the spiritual aspects of the body and ignore other areas will often drive a wounded, hungry, sick, and/or lonely person to seek care outside the safety of the church. The *Pastoral Care Diagram* below demonstrates the possibilities of pastoral care that should be contemplated when extending care.

Pastoral Care Diagram

Method of Care (Narrative)	Interpretation of Care Given/Needed	Outcomes/Goals of Care (Breadth)	Facets of Care (Holistic)
God's Story			
Caregiver's Story	Tradition	Healing	Spiritual
Care Receiver's Story	Culture	Sustaining	Physical
	Community	Guiding	Mental
	Familial/ Individual	Reconciling	Emotional
		Resisting	Relational
		Empowering	Social
		Liberating	Logistical

A Pastoral Care Model

A Narrative Method

A narrative method of pastoral care provides a simple method to assess and interpret the stories and experiences of those seeking care. Interpreting the stories of care seekers allows caregivers to set outcomes/goals that wholly encompass all human needs. If the caregiver makes no effort to hear the stories of the care seeker, the resulting care often results in providing care that does not meet the need and appears unfamiliar, unpalatable, ineffective, and unsustainable. Further, when the voices of the silent speak (caregivers are encouraged to share their own story), one can also hear the still, small voices of the Spirit and the Word that demonstrate how the story of care seekers combine with God's grand narrative to love and redeem the world. Seeing one's story combined with God's story gives transformative power in the light and revelation of the broader Christian story in ways that are understandable.[2]

Pastoral caregivers must listen deeply to the stories of those often deprived of voice, "believing whatever she says and allowing her to name and define the problems she experiences, creates a novelty that in itself empowers and strengthens."[3] Good listening empowers care seekers to tell the story that names the pain, names the fear, names whatever you wish to name, empowers, strengthens, and makes new creation real and possible. "The purpose of gaining voice [telling one's story] is not to drown out those other voices in the community, but to enable all to be co-authors and co-creators with each other and with God."[4] Nothing will draw care seekers closer to God, closer to the body of Christ, to healing, and to his beauty than when one is invited to tell their story and become one with the story-telling God as part of his on-going creation.

Quite simply, the narrative method of the pastoral care model occurs while giving, sharing, telling, and listening to stories (by both care seeker and caregiver) in the illuminating light and power of God's own story! The sharing and exploring of the care seeker's story, illuminated in the light of God's story and the caregiver's story, facilitates the *interpretation* of pastoral care needed, determines the *outcomes/goals* of pastoral care provided, and ensures the holistic incorporation of all *facets* of pastoral care. For a more

2. Doehring, *Practice of Pastoral*, xiv–xvi.
3. Neuger, *Counseling Women*, 71–92.
4. Neuger, *Counseling Women*, 71–92.

complete explanation of a narrative pastoral care method, consult *Pastoral Care: Telling the Stories of Our Lives* by Karen Scheib.

Interpretation of Care

Charles Gerkin's interpretive pastoral care model emphasizes the importance of inviting care seekers to participate with caregivers to determine the care needed. When utilizing his four-part model—*traditions, culture, community,* and *familial*—listening to the care seeker's story/problem informs the caregiver of what is influencing the situation (See Table 1[5] below for definitions of the individual elements of the Gerkin's model). Proper *interpretation* requires caregivers to listen deeply to the *traditions, cultures, communities,* and *familial* influences of the care seeker. Focused listening by the caregiver provides a safe and transparent environment amid suffering, grief, confusion, and hopelessness. When the caregiver takes the time to listen to the care seeker(s)' story and reflects with them in the light of God's story, care seeker(s) are more likely to receive the care needed and not the presupposed care that the caregiver might otherwise bring from his own experience/education. This hallowed place of listening and absorbing creates community, welcomes the work of the Holy Spirit to bring peace, belonging, and comfort to a confused and displaced world. While working in this sacred, communal space where the Holy Spirit dwells, the caregiver can look for opportunities to set goals for the appropriate pastoral care in a holistic manner, neither strange nor foreign. When listening to the care seeker's *traditions, culture, community, and family*, the caregiver's *traditions, culture, community, and family,* can join *traditions,* share *cultures,* combine *communities,* as one *family* with God. For a more complete understanding of the influences of pastoral care interpretation, consult *An Introduction to Pastoral Care* by Charles Gerkin.

5. Peyton, *Modern Exodus*, 96.

Influencers	Definitions
Traditions	The method(s) in which customs, beliefs (including religious beliefs and sacred texts), understanding, stories, rules, heritage, etc. (spoken and unspoken) is passed down, spread, and/or repeated from one generation to another generation. Tradition is the totem (present and past) of how experiential influences are understood and handed down.
Culture	The existing manifestation of the collective intellectual achievements that influences the collective. All (good or bad, moral or immoral, known and unknown) that currently influence any aspect of one's life is culture.
Community	A group of people living in relatively close proximity that have certain common social, physical, traditional, religious, historic, ethnical, and cultural characteristics, physiognomies, rules, and beliefs. A community exists around commonality!
Familial	The immediate family and the individual members of one's genetic microcosm into which they live, function, and find support. Family is the collection/collaboration of individuals that maintain their own traditions and cultures as a community within other larger communities.

Table 1—Definitions of the Elements of Interpretation

Outcomes/Goals of Care

Pastoral care should follow the elements of the classical pastoral care model of *healing, sustaining, guiding, reconciling, resisting, empowering,* and *liberating* (see definitions in Table 2[6] below for definitions of the individual elements). As one listens to a care seeker's story, a story set in their *traditions, culture, community,* and *familial* influences, the caregiver sets goals/outcomes of *healing, sustaining, guiding, reconciling, resisting, empowering,* and/or *liberating.* Exploration through stories enables caregivers to determine the specific needs and set specific outcomes/goals, because few, if any, need care in all seven of these elements at the same time, which again emphasizes the need for deep listening to the stories at hand. However, pastoral caregivers must look for occasions to teach and/or provide preventive care (education) in each of the classical emphases in a church setting. Caregivers must avoid the temptation to presume the needs of others and set the outcomes/goals without really listening. Only when taking time for

6. Peyton, *Modern Exodus,* 98.

in-depth encounters between pastoral caregivers and care seekers, can one correctly interpret the care needed and set the appropriate outcomes/goals. For more information on understanding the specific elements and/or the setting of outcomes/goals of care, consult the *Dictionary of Pastoral Care and Counseling*, edited by Rodney Hunter and Nancy Ramsay.

Outcomes/ Goals	Definitions
Healing	"The process of being restored to bodily wholeness, emotional well-being, mental functioning, and spiritual aliveness."[7]
Sustaining	"To console and strengthen; to stand alongside, to lend support and encouragement when the situation cannot be changed, at least not immediately; to carry on a ministry of sustenance as long as circumstance precludes healing."[8]
Guiding	"The act of helping a person find their way through an unfamiliar, confusing, or difficult situation, often in which some kind of decision making is involved, as in solving family problems, making life decisions, or pursuing a spiritual discipline."[9]
Reconciling	"The establishment of harmony with one's world, one's destiny, or one-self . . . seeks to reestablish broken relationships with others, including God."[10]
Resisting	"Resistance signals our human agency for change, particularly when we work together in diverse coalitions to support neighbors and strangers. Resistance is oppositional, it involves using human agency for change to oppose something" (attentive to postcolonial realities, responding to injustice, space for resistance movements, and allows for authentic participation).[11]
Empowering	Empowering is a communal affair that includes: "working together with people to attempt to restore community spirit; trying to make governments more responsive to people's needs; encouraging groups based on one or another identity issue; political education and consciousness-raising; organizing user or service groups and encouraging groups to develop their own alternative economic power base."[12]

7. Graham, *Healing*, 497.

8. Aden, *Comfort/Sustaining*, 195.

9. Mitchell, *Guidance, Pastoral*, 486.

10. Burck, *Community, Fellowship, Care*, 1047.

11. Sharp, *Creating Resistances*, 4.

12. Lartey, *Pastoral Theology*, 68.

Outcomes/ Goals	Definitions
Liberating	"Liberating involves the intricate and delicate processes of raising awareness about the sources and causes of oppression and domination in society . . . the critical and analytic examining of both personal and structural sources, causes and developments in the establishment of current situations of inequality . . . [and] the need for choice and action followed by reflection and evaluation."[13]

Table 2—Definition of the Elements of Outcomes/Goals

Facets of Care

When exploring (*interpreting*) the story/problem/situation of a care seeker, and while determining the *outcomes/goals* required/desired, the caregiver must also holistically consider every *facet* of what it means to be human (*spiritual, physical, mental, emotional, social, relational,* and *logistical*) (see definitions in Table 3[14] below for definitions of the individual elements). To consider in isolation one *facet of care,* e.g., an emotional need—often more visible due to an external demonstration—or a spiritual need (because that is what the church is all about), often results in the church ignoring an underlying physical, logistical, and/or mental obstacle. Therefore, "the holistic approach requires [exploration and/or] action to be taken in the widest sense of the word, because the [holistic] approach includes all that might be needed to develop empowerment and to enhance change."[15]

Isolating care to a single *facet* creates a dualism that minimizes the entirety of what it means to be created in the image of God. Rather, because every human exists as one "whole" person, caregivers must explore all facets of the one "whole" person treated. Caregivers must avoid jumping to conclusions, because presenting issues often mask the discovery without consideration to the whole spectrum of care that could be discovered while listening to one's long and complex story. For more information on approaching pastoral care holistically, consult *A Holistic Approach to Pastoral Care and Poverty* in the journal *Verbum et Ecclesia* by Johan Janse Van Rensburg.

13. Lartey, *Pastoral Theology,* 67.

14. Peyton, *Modern Exodus,* 100.

15. Janse van Rensburg, *Holistic Approach,* 1.

Facets of Care	Definitions
Spiritual	This will mean something different to different people. For example, the *Dictionary of Pastoral Care and Counselling* breaks down spirituality definitions into Christian and non-Christian; then Christian is divided into Orthodox, Protestant, and Catholic; and then Protestant is broken down into secular, evangelical, charismatic, ecumenical, oriental, etc. Basically, spirituality is "to be understood as taking place within the household of faith" and is referring to one's "devotion or piety" to their faith.[16] The pastoral care concerns are with the spiritual well-being of whatever one considers their spiritual life.
Physical	Physical refers "to the body as opposed to the mind."[17] The pastoral care concerns are with the physical well-being of one's health: current health care, prophylactic health care, and overall physical fitness care.
Mental	Mental refers to maladies that pertain to the mind: biological diseases, gestation malformations, kinetic or chemical injuries, and/or a wide range of mental disabilities. The pastoral care concerns are with the mental well-being of the care seeker and providing a space for their full inclusion in the life of the church.
Emotional	Emotion refers to the "instinctive state of mind deriving from one's circumstances, mood, or relationships with others."[18] Usually thought of in the negative, such as grief, sadness, loneliness, horror, belonging, etc., but care can also be needed at times with happiness, joy, exuberance, ecstasy, etc. The pastoral care concerns are with the emotional well-being of the care seeker and providing a safe place for the emotions to be expressed and/or processed.
Relational	Relational refers to "the way in which two or more people or groups feel about and behave toward each other."[19] The pastoral care concerns are with relational well-being in the way individuals connect, relate, respond to others: e.g., spouses, friends, pastors, coworkers, community members, parishioners, etc.
Social	Social care refers to caring for those effected by social change, social dislocation, social development, social isolation, social depravity, and social injustice. The pastoral care concerns are with the social well-being of groups and individuals by promoting social consciousness, social responsibility, and assisting with access to social services.

16. Hunter and Ramsey, *Dictionary of Pastoral*, 1213–24.
17. Oxford, *Physical*, 2020.
18. Oxford, *Emotional*, 2020.
19. Oxford, *Relational*, 2020.

Facets of Care	Definitions
Logistical	Logistical care refers to pastoral care concerns with the removal of logistical barriers that prevent the well-being in other areas: e.g., church attendance, education, transportation, housing, access, language, etc.

Table 3—Definition of Elements of Facets of Care

Who Provides Pastoral Care? The Priesthood of All Believers

Before we consider the specific relationship between the second commandment and pastoral care, it is important to identify who should be the providers of pastoral care. Over the last two thousand years, caring for the body of Christ has increasingly been limited to a select few individuals (pastors, counselors, etc.) and in some cases this may be a wise choice. However, much of pastoral care is as simple as presence (being there), listening, fellowship, friendship, assisting the elderly and/or disabled, and encouragement. Unfortunately, many local churches still expect their pastor to be the sole provider of pastoral care instead of the equipper/organizer of the laity to provide care.

The Bible portrays pastoral care differently, as the work of many. Only in modern times has the single caregiver idea made its way into church polity. The parable of the shepherd in John 10:6–18, regardless of one's ability to twist the text, cannot substantiate an elitist form of clericalism. Jesus did not regard his disciples as merely sheep to follow ignorantly or simply be guarded by a superior being. Rather, for just under three years, he trained the uneducated and untrained (Acts 4:13) and then sent them into the world as his representatives and witnesses (Matt 10:5–15). Jesus trained the sheep to go forth as the shepherds in the new kingdom. As well, the Great Commission in Matt 28:19 instructed them (the disciples) to go and make disciples, and in John 13:15 Jesus directed them to repeat the cycle of ministry in the same manner Jesus demonstrated in his earthly ministry.

Pastoral care exists as a partnership between God, as the Great Shepherd, and the people of God, as the sheep, collectively shepherding (caring for) the whole community. Varied members of the body of Christ may possess specific responsibilities based upon gifting, but the whole body jointly nurtures, comforts, and edifies one another together (1 Thess 5:11). Pastoral care coexists as both personal (one-on-one) and corporate (by the whole body of Christ) "to the end that the community is enabled and empowered, not only to live and work to God's praise and glory, but to reach out to those outside its boundaries and so advance the kingdom of God."[20]

The importance lies in reinforcing the need for the church to break the clerical monopoly on ministry and argue for "a ministry in which all God's people participate."[21] The vast amount of pastoral care needed generates a tremendous burden on the field of pastoral care, especially if one argues for holistic care among all people as a biblical mandate. This will never happen "as long as the members of the church are unable to work together," and, consequently, the world will remain untouched by the church's efforts.[22] The needs of the church and the community (the potential church), the skills needed in caregivers so varied, and the differences are so immense, that the burden of pastoral care must be carried by the whole church caring/reaching for the whole world.

Pastoral Care, The Second Commandment, and a Biblical Defense

The truths of the biblical text demonstrated in the pastoral care experience is based upon the very nature of God and includes his care and love for the world. God's willingness to give/sacrifice his only son on the cross as the payment for the sins of humanity establishes his loving and caring nature (John 3:16–17). However, the journey to the cross and the illustration of his love/care for the world, did not start at the cross, in a manger, or even at the advent of the New Testament; rather, it started with, "In the beginning God created the heaven and the earth" (Gen 1:1). "The entire canon shows a concern with human well-being with reference to God."[23] Consequently, to fully understand God's caring nature, his love for the world, and his desire to be loved, one must recognize the road to redemption began at creation.

"In the beginning . . ." when God created humankind and the world in which they would live, the uniqueness of God's imagination was shown by the vast array of individuality in each of his creative acts (Gen 1). However, on the sixth day, after uniquely creating many things, God does the first non-unique act of the entire creation: God created humanity in his own image (Gen 1:26). In creating humans in his own image, and

20. Burfield, *Identifying Pastoral Care*, 149.

21. Deeks, *Pastoral Theology*, 252.

22. Elmer, *Cross-Cultural Servanthood*, 77.

23. Johnson, *Foundations*, 29.

the creation of the Garden of Eden in which his image/creation would live, one sees God's nature affectionately demonstrated. In the early days before the fall, God's image/nature is seen in Adam's commission to work and care for the Garden. This command, "to rule over and care for the earth . . . ascribes to man a relationship found in no other creatures, not even angels,"[24] a relationship made possible only because of the "likeness" and/or mirroring of man's nature to God's.

Consequently, what is fundamental to providing pastoral care today ensues when caregivers mirror God's own image/nature in their love for the care receiver. Pastoral care is based upon the relationship between people who care and people who need care. This need/command to love and care for others stands essential to pastoral care theology. God's ongoing care for humanity is put in the hands of caregivers and should arise from God's compassion and/or nature. The first two chapters of Genesis contain only the beginning of the story of God's love for the world. The need for pastoral care becomes increasingly important after humanity separates from God's presence. Genesis chapter 3, and the rest of the Old Testament, tells the story of the fall and the consequential need for redemption by the God who loved enough to pay the ultimate price for that care with the life of his son.

The attack of the serpent in the garden, assaulting the very nature/ image of God, also damaged his plan to care for the world he created. Even though the fall fractured the image God created and disfigured God's nature in the world, the fallen man still bears God's image. As with a broken mirror, it no longer "images God properly, and therefore must again be restored to the image of God."[25] Until the day of redemption, when the seed of the woman arose and bruised the head of the serpent, pastoral caregivers attended to the search for redemption. Old Testament people of God strived to bridge the vast canyon between God and his broken image. Especially important in the giving of the law was the premise, "Thou shalt love thy neighbor as thyself: I am the Lord" (Lev 19:18). Despite the efforts in the Old Testament to bridge the gap created by the fall, the deeds of the law could never justify flesh in the sight of God (Rom 3:20) and existed only as "our schoolmaster [guardian] to bring us unto Christ, that we might be justified by faith" (Gal 3:24).

The coming of Christ and the New Testament covenant involved a change from Law written on tablets of clay to law written in the heart (Jer

24. Hoekema, *Created*, 81.
25. Hoekema, *Created*, 72.

31:31–34; 32:38–40; Ezek 36:25–32). This new birth restores humanity to the nature of God in ways that Old Testament caregivers could never imagine. The fusion of God's nature written on the hearts of humankind would no longer isolate the love and care of neighbor to brethren, but would extend to the least of these (Matt 25:45), to one's enemies (Luke 6:27, 35), and to any that were near and in need (Luke 10:25–37). Jesus came not to abolish the law, but he fulfilled the law (Matt 5:17) when he revealed that the intention of the law was the restoration of his nature— his love/care for his creation—which was the basis of all the law and the prophets (Matt 22:36–40). "For all the law is fulfilled in one word . . . Thou shalt love thy neighbor as thyself" (Gal 5:14).

The loving of one's neighbor taught in the New Testament embodies the nature of God and the restoration of the very nature of God in believers. Thomas Merton stated, "What we are asked to do at present is not so much to speak of Christ as to let him live in us so that people may find him by feeling how he lives in us."[26] The essence of the new covenant restores the nature of Christ (Rom 3:27; 13:14) which includes the restoration of the very image of God in the lives of the converted: humility, gentleness, patience, (Acts 4:1–21), care for the disadvantaged (1 Thess 5:14; Jas 1:27), listening (Jas 1:19), freedom from anxiety (Phil 4:6), bearing other's burdens (Gal 6:2), and a radical love for humanity (Eph 4:2; 1 Cor 13). In other words, believers, "as a new creation in Christ through the work of the Holy Spirit, is called to be conformed to Jesus, who is himself the very image of God" (Col 1:15; 2 Cor 4:4).[27] Therefore, the doctrine regarding the image of God is fundamental to pastoral care and ultimately "to all pastoral work in the church."[28] Fundamental to the image of God is his love for humanity.

The Pastoral Care Method and the Second Commandment

The narrative method used with the model includes the intersecting of God's story (his love for the world), the caregiver's story (the story of the redeemed), and the care receiver's story (the story of those being redeemed). Caregivers participate in receiving and giving love to their neighbors, seeking justice and completeness for all the world (restoring God's image), and learn to live life with the fullness of both. The first and

26. Flemming, *Recovering*, 264.

27. Hobson, *Imago Dei*, xvii.

28. Hobson, *Imago Dei*, xvii.

the second commandments (love for God and love for people), all within a caring relationship, embodies the wisdom of God that brings healing and hope to a broken world.

Standing alone, caregivers have little to offer the broken and hurting who are most often not much different than themselves. Likewise, the biblical text appears distant, unrelatable, and unapproachable by the likes of fallen humanity. However, narrative pastoral care allows the caregiver to merge the stories of the Scripture with the broken stories of the care seeker and the caregiver. The stories combine to create a new narrative that leads to positive outcomes. In essence then, the blending of narratives, the making of one story out of many stories, is the sum of the new kingdom of God.

The Pastoral Care Model and the Second Commandment

The chaos of history contains the constant changing/evolving of pastoral care methodology and models, change that has increased over the last one hundred years. However, increasingly apparent in these shifts are two unchanging themes that underpin each adjustment to pastoral care: humanity's creation in God's image and loving care demonstrated by God's actions in the world. Pastoral care is the newly created kingdom of God with mutual care and love for one another (2 Cor 6:16); it is the body of Christ with unique gifts and ministry for the body of Christ (all for all) (Rom 12:4–5; 1 Cor 10:17); and it is a Spirit-empowered kingdom where the Spirit works to bring care to a broken world (Acts 10: 44–47). Therefore, this model insists that caregivers see care seekers as the image of God (*interpretation of care*); provide all *facets of care* in emulation of God's nature by allowing the whole body/image of Christ to exercise their unique gifts and ministries; and the recognition—and allowance—of the Spirit in orchestrating *outcomes/goals of care*.

Interpretation of Care and the Second Commandment

Father, I will that they also, whom thou hast given me, be with me where I am; that they may behold my glory, which thou hast given me: for thou lovedst me before the foundation of the world. O righteous Father, the world hath not known thee: but I have known thee, and these have known that thou hast sent me. And I have declared unto them thy name, and will declare it: that the love wherewith thou hast loved me may be in them, and I in them (John 17:24–26).

The desire to be known and to know others is rooted in the nature and the relationship of the Godhead (John 10:15). Care based upon love of neighbors shows believers that if they pursue such knowing (John 8:19; 14:7) they too can enjoy such a relationship with God and humanity. It was because the son knew the Father that he, by extension, would know humanity and lay down his life (John 10:15). The pursuit by humanity to know and be known was broken in the fall. As Paul said, "For now we see through a glass, darkly," but the same passage promises that in the pursuit of God, someday we will see him "face to face" where we will be fully known (1 Cor 13:12). In the pursuit of peace with his brother, the Old Testament patriarch Jacob came face-to-face with God at Jabbok's ford, and, in a sense, there he knew God for the first time (Gen 32:30). Then, because he knew God, Jacob saw the face of God in the face of his brother, and for the first time really knew his brother (Gen 33:10). Fundamentally, the nature of God, given to humanity in creation, broken in the fall, and restored on the cross, connects life with this pursuit to know and be known.

An *interpretation of care* brings understanding—knowing—to the relationship junction between caregiver, care seeker, and the God that created them. During such efforts, caregivers receive background information, consider unknown issues, and discover solutions. At the same time, the care seeker receives information about the story of the redemption of the caregiver. Both caregiver and care seeker recognize how their overlapping stories receive life through God's Spirit as their joint stories blend as part of God's narrative. This collaborative knowing, between pastoral care and the biblical story, will "inform, correct, and guide the practice of the caregiving art, while this practice brings to life basic biblical truths as they become incarnate in caregiving relationships."[29]

While the early church caregivers, because of their state of unknowing, struggled with the acceptance of gentile influences into their midst, the biblical text clearly demonstrates the position of the Holy Spirit, "What God hath cleansed, that call not thou common" (Acts 10:15). The church elders, because of their unknowing, struggled with Peter's obvious efforts to provide care. However, when they knew that the Gentiles had received the Spirit in the same manner as the disciples on the Day of Pentecost (heard their story), James responded to the opposition, "Forasmuch then as God gave them the

29. Clinebell, *Basic Types*, 45.

like gift as he did unto us, who believed on the Lord Jesus Christ; what was I, that I could withstand God" (Acts 11:17). The broad question of knowing was settled by James, speaking for the Jerusalem council, "Wherefore my sentence is, that we trouble not them, which from among the Gentiles are turned to God" (Acts 15:19). This narrative demonstrates the interaction between the caregivers, Peter, Paul, Silas, and others; the care seekers, Gentiles coming into the new church; and the Holy Spirit establishing God's will and mission in the lives of a knowing and caring people.

Outcomes/Goals of Care and the Second Commandment

While considering the *interpretation of care,* caregivers must consider a broad range of *outcomes/goals (healing, sustaining, guiding, reconciling, resisting, empowering,* and/or *liberating).* Pastoral care is an expression of God's love to embody Christ-like care in underprivileged communities, caring for a full range of human needs. In the first century of the church, care included more than spiritual matters: taxes paid (Matt 17:27), widows fed (Acts 6:1–2), comfort given in tribulation (2 Cor 1:4), liberation (Luke 4:18), collection of finances for others (1 Cor 16:1–4), etc.

Most important, the pursuit of a full range of outcomes/goals when providing pastoral care should resolve, or at least minimize, many of the misunderstandings, misinterpretations, and misapplications that arise from caring in a vacuum of ignorance (unknowing). The story of the Good Samaritan (Luke 10:25–37) demonstrated such a range of outcomes/goals: caring for the injuries (*healing*), carrying the victim on his beast (*sustaining*), and taking the victim to a place where he could be cared for (*guiding*). The early church's narrow focus of salvific/spiritual care created a misunderstanding and murmuring (*liberating* and *empowering*) among the Grecians (*resisting*) when their widows needed food (*reconciling*) (Acts 6:1). When caregivers take the time to consider a full range of *outcomes/goals,* they lower barriers created by misunderstandings and build bridges across "the many canyons that divide the human family."[30]

---

30. Clinebell, *Basic Types,* 414.

Facets of Care and the Second Commandment

Pastoral caregivers cannot separate the *facets of care* as if they exist separately, "since man is a whole person, the spiritual and the mental aspects of a totality . . . [who] influences and is influenced by the other . . . [t]he church must be concerned about the whole person."[31] "There is no exhaustive list of what the church must do; rather the church must remain open to respond to any human needs that arise."[32] At the time of Christ's first miracle, turning water into wine (John 2:1–11), Christ demonstrated his willingness to engage socially, more than just spiritual involvement, with the Hebrew culture. In fact, "the entire ministry of Jesus was without distinction between the spiritual and the physical, nor between the temporal and the eternal."[33]

From the beginning, God's creation included all the *facets* of God's image: one sees God's ability to walk in the Garden (*physical*), the aptitude to converse and reason with the serpent (*spiritual* and *mental*), the recognition that it was not good for Adam to exist alone (*social* and *relational*), the capacity to love Eve (*emotional*), and the capability to care for the Garden (*logistical*) (Gen 1–2). In short, God created humanity in his own likeness so that they could bear his image in their very nature. Adam and Eve were stamped with his image, not for their own pleasure, but in their God-given nature to live fully and fruitfully while replenishing the earth (Gen 1:28) and caring for the Garden in which they lived (Gen 2:15). The image of God must include all facets of what it means to be structurally and functionally human.

The serpent attacked God's dependability, veracity, and faithfulness in a way that questioned all the *facets* of God's being/image (Gen 3:1–6). It was as if the serpent said to Eve, "God is not who you think he is!" and, by extension, "If God is not who you think he is, then you are not who you think you are!" Adam and Eve's willingness to embrace the lies of the serpent fractured the very essence of their being, the created image of God. "To be human is to be the image of God. It is not an extra feature added on to our species; it is definitive of what it means to be human."[34] Pastoral care aids in the ongoing restoration of the full *facets* of God's image (*physically, spiritually, emotionally, mentally, relationally, socially, and logistically*) in the life of his creation.

31. Hoekema, *Created*, 222, 225.
32. Chuga, *Wholistic Ministry*, 15.
33. Chuga, *Wholistic Ministry*, 11.
34. Wright, *Mission of God*, 421.

Lessons Learned at the Intersection of Pastoral Care
and the Second Commandment

No lesson could be more important than discovering that God's nature (his love and care for humanity) began with the creation of all things and continues throughout the biblical timeline. Biblical caregivers emulated the nature of God, and/or God rebuked caregivers when they failed to provide the care his nature mandated. God's nature can be demonstrated in each element of the pastoral care model (*interpretation of care*, the *outcomes/goals of care*, and the *facets of care*). Further, the biblical timeline connects the thread of God's nature to the birth of the New Testament church: the creation of humanity in his image (Gen 1:26–28); the call of Abraham to bless the nations (Gen 12:1–3); the (re)circumcision of Israel by Joshua, linking them to the Mosaic Law and the Abrahamic Covenant (Josh 5); assuring the Babylonian diaspora of their restoration as God's people—including a shower of blessings for those gathered around the people of God (Ezek 36:26–31); commissioning the Christian diaspora to go and teach all nations (Matt 28:19); and the reminder to the early church that as the seed of Abraham, the heirs of his calling, and as followers of Jesus, they must emulate God's nature and live as a blessing to all nations (Acts 3:25–26).

Such threads, seen throughout the biblical record, contain the core of the Bible's mission—the restoration/redemption of humans as the image of God in the world. The Bible's command to be a blessing cannot be separated from the Great Commission—go and teach all nations—or the great commandments: love God, love your neighbor. Ancient caregivers provided pastoral care in emulation of God's nature that was founded upon this foundation (be a blessing to all nations, go and teach all nations, and do so while loving God/loving others). The idea that this heritage still exists today remains the foundation on which all pastoral care must occur.

> *Pastor Levi sat in his office thinking about what he had learned about pastoral care. He knew that he had never really done anything that even closely resembled the pastoral care model. As he sat there pondering what to do, he realized that anything he would do must start with an assessment, and an assessment must start with listening. But where to start? After he thought about it awhile, he determined that Jim and Sharon's marriage was probably the most pressing issue. So, he got in his car and went over to their house. Unfortunately, there was no one home.*

As he stood on the porch, he tried hard not to be frustrated or mad at God. God seemed to be teaching him many things about caring and loving others, yet after prayerfully working up the courage to reach out to Jim and Sharon, nobody was home. As he stood there, he noticed an old lady sitting on the neighboring porch. When she realized that he saw her, she called out to him, "Jim is still at work and Sharon is at the store." Pastor Levi crossed the lawn, so he didn't have to raise his voice when greeting Sally, and introduced himself. Sally invited Pastor Levi to sit in the other chair on the porch and wait for someone to return next door. For a while they made small talk, with Sally doing most of the talking.

As he sat and listened, he began to realize how easy it was to guide Sally as she told her story. Sally remembered attending Methodist camp meetings that came through the area about seventy years ago. She wondered if the things she had heard about Pastor Levi's church were like those old camp meetings. Sally reminisced of being a life-long member of the Community Church in town with her husband. At least she was until her husband—her ride to church— had died ten years before. The Community Church now only had services once a month, and it had been over five years since anyone had thought to check on Sally or offer her a ride to church. As Pastor Levi listened, he began to pick out the important pieces and do an assessment: husband's death (family); life-long member of the Community Church; faith established in a camp meeting a long time ago (traditions); services once a week . . . no one remembering an old lady (culture). Maybe this was pastoral care . . . maybe he could do more than just preach in a pulpit.

Pastor Levi began identifying possible outcomes/goals based upon what he was hearing. As Sally talked about how much she missed going to church, he offered her a ride to church (empowering). By just sitting on her porch and listening, he realized that he was sustaining her life of faith. When he offered to come back again and give her a Bible study, she accepted so fast that he had to laugh in delight (guiding). After an hour, that included prayer for Sally's arthritis, Pastor Levi had to leave, since neither Jim nor Sharon had returned. He realized that he had provided care in four areas: the ride to church (logistical); the listening (social, relational); and the plan to teach the Bible Study and the prayer (spiritual). Pastor Levi drove down the street with tears running down his cheeks! Maybe . . . just maybe, God had known what he was doing when he sent him to Jim and Sharon's empty house.

7

The Second Commandment
in Christian Education

So after he had washed their feet, and had taken his garments,
and was set down again, he said unto them, Know ye what I
have done to you? Ye call me Master and Lord: and ye say well;
for so I am. If I then, your Lord and Master, have washed your
feet; ye also ought to wash one another's feet. *For I have given
you an example, that ye should do as I have done to you.*
Verily, verily, I say unto you, The servant is not greater than his
lord; neither he that is sent greater than he that sent him. If ye
know these things, happy are ye if ye do them.

—JOHN 13:12–17[1]

*Hand in hand they walked together, Jim and his first-born son.
Jim walked with long, grownup strides, while Billy ran to match
his steps. There was no rulebook or classroom lecture that taught
Billy to walk like his father. There were no lessons that taught him
to wear his ball cap with the same slant as Dad's cap, nor to stick
his free hand deep into his suit pants pocket, just as where Dad kept
his hand. Soon Billy will grow up, and when he is grown, people
will remark on how much he is just like Jim. As a man, Billy will
sit with his family and bless the food; the prayer will sound a whole
lot like his father's prayers used to sound; that is, he will if Jim can*

---

1. Emphasis added.

*keep his family together and prays where Billy can hear him. You
see, Billy is Daddy's boy.*

*Most can remember the first time Betty came to church. Her
sins were gross, and her life was a mess. She worked with Jim, but
Jim had not invited her. Her visit was the result of a chance meeting
in a grocery store with Jane, Pastor Levi's wife. On her first visit,
some wondered if Betty would ever make the grade and become a
good Christian. That first night, someone saw her look at Jane on the
other side of the church. They looked so different; one redeemed and
the other so desperate for redemption. God is merciful, and Betty
claimed salvation at the foot of an old rugged cross that night. Betty
began to change over the next few years, but one thing slowly became
apparent to all. Betty began to look like someone they all knew. Her
clothing styles, her worship, and her testimonies were familiar and
possessed a recognizable ring. They may have never discovered of
whom she reminded everyone if Jim and Sharon had not sat in Jane's
seat one night. The only seat left for Jane was next to Betty, and then
they knew the rest of the story. Jane had never taught a lesson to
Betty on how to dress or live, yet Betty was imitating Jane and Jane
was mentoring Betty (intentionally or not).*

LONG BEFORE THE FIRST teacher stepped to the front of the classroom
and opened her lesson book, people were already learning. Before the
first school or the first college degree, folks were already being educated.
Children watched their parents, peers watched each other, others watched
mentors, and knowledge was learned within the community in which
people lived. There is little doubt that Christian education can positively
interface with, and is affected by, the second commandment. "A theory
of Christian education must include a strong component of modeling
and imitation, because these are biblical methods of instruction and are
in agreement with how God has designed people to learn."[2] Without the
proximity required while loving one's neighbor, the opportunity for biblical modeling and Christ-like imitation is greatly limited.

In this chapter, the author will first explain the effect that second commandment ministry can have upon the Christian educational experience.
Second, it will demonstrate that the learning environment is positively influenced by a community that loves their neighbor. Third, several examples
of how community empowers learning will be demonstrated. Fourth, the

2. Downs, *Teaching*, 164.

Bible will speak on the role of Christian education and a community created by second commandment ministry. Finally, the responsibilities outlined by second commandment principles (love God, love neighbor) will establish the biblical model for Christian education.

The church has been accused (and rightly so, sometimes) of being in the "huddle syndrome" and only looking inward with no thought or inclination to reach out to influence the world around them. If a New Testament revival is to happen in the twenty-first century, the church must burst out of the huddle with a game plan that presents the church to the world as a community of believers. The words of St. Augustine, over fifteen hundred years ago, still beckon to us today: "Attract them by your way of life if you want them to receive . . . teaching from you . . . it is the only way to cause the world to take seriously our protestations concerning truth."[3]

Community Interfaces with Christian Education

A popular saying at the end of the twentieth century was, "Me and Jesus got our own thing going." Nothing could be further from the truth, and nothing could be less biblical than man presenting himself as a loner with God. The Bible teaches, while the church is made up of many members, together they are but one body in Christ (1 Cor 12:19–21). Humanity is not designed to grow and learn alone; rather educational experiences are most successful when undertaken within the bosom of society.

If this is true of education in general, it is increasingly true within the realm of Christian education. "Christians are not to be solitary creatures. By learning in community, we begin to learn how to live in community. Also, the community provides one of the best learning environments as people with similar struggles and stories can come alongside and point us to the hope that lies in Christ."[4] From the early writings of the church, one finds that second commandment ministry (fellowship and community) played a major role in the creation of both the first church and the educating of the first Christians (Acts 2:42).

Community building is a powerful motivation. This point is missed in many churches today, as they try one program after another. Without realizing that community building is found at the point of loving God and loving one's neighbor, there is often no motivation for church members to

3. Dockery and Gushee, *Future*, 137.
4. Wilhoit and Dettoni, *Nuture*, 23.

do or learn anything. The Bible, sitting unread and unapplied on a shelf, is empty and without meaning. But within a community, the Bible becomes alive and motivates the church to both love God and love neighbor as salt and light in the world. Proclamation of the gospel cannot exist without a community to hear, and community cannot stand without a commitment to love one's neighbor. Unfortunately, many do not see the interrelated dependency of the gospel and the second commandment—both require community to exist.

Learning Environments are Influenced by the Community

> Hear, O Israel: The LORD our God is one LORD: And thou shalt love the LORD thy God with all thine heart, and with all thy soul, and with all thy might. And these words, which I command thee this day, shall be in thine heart: And thou shalt teach them diligently unto thy children, and shalt talk of them when thou sittest in thine house, and when thou walkest by the way, and when thou liest down, and when thou risest up (Deut 6:4–7).

From the first moments after the giving of the law, God was concerned with the educational environment of the Hebrew children. This emphasis was an obvious necessity in God's desire for an ongoing heritage between himself and the Hebrews. In the home, out of the home, when they were up and about, and when they were taking it easy; there was not to be a time when the parents could relax and take time off from educating their children. This educational environment was not a formal classroom with books and whiteboards on which to write their lessons. No, a Hebrew child learned to worship, respect God, and love the Torah because their parents were members of a community that worshiped, respected God, and loved the Torah.[5]

No learning environment is more influenced by the community than the educational community of a child. To separate a child's community from his education would be the same as eliminating his education entirely and destroying his ability to grow in a healthy, God-ordained environment. Unfortunately, many churches are constantly trying to educate their spiritual and/or natural children separate from the community, a community formed by a group of people that are committed to loving their neighbors. "Most of what children learn occurs through their natural tendency to

---

5. Pazmino, *Foundational Issues*, 130–32.

imitate or model the behavior of others."[6] A child's community includes parents, caretakers, relatives, schoolteachers, and children's ministry workers. God designed each child with a built-in tendency to imitate the important people that make up their community.

As well, if a child is affected by the community, by extension, the family is equally affected. If the child's community (family) is acting in a manner that is positively influencing the child by a worthy, godly example, it can't help but affect the whole family. Therefore, "the home should be viewed as the primary agency of Christian education."[7] Even further, the family is a smaller element of the larger community that also affects the life of the child. The family must affect its larger community by its godly commitment to community. "The family, functioning as a small unit of the Body of Christ, can influence the [larger] community by its example."[8]

Peer relationships are one form of community (such as an entire graduating class or groups of friends) that have a powerful impact on learning. The day-to-day relationships of peers can have a positive effect on each other while they learn to care, pray, and love one another, as opposed to pick on, criticize, or condemn one another. In other words, when peers learn to love their neighbor as themselves, the community created by obedience to the second commandment will have a positive educational effect on each one. "And the LORD turned the captivity of Job, when he prayed for his friends: also the LORD gave Job twice as much as he had before" (Job 42:10). Although people of all ages are affected by their peers, "teenagers tend to be heavily influenced by their peer groups."[9]

One form of peer grouping in the church is when students are grouped together by age and/or education level. Students learn better from their peers, because with their peers they identify and relax better than with a teacher or pastor. These communities of peers increase learning, and many schools are making peer-learning communities a major strategy for building a better education system. Hence the church is the schoolhouse of one's spirit, and therefore the church must become more than a repository of money and become obedient to the Bible's call to faithfulness to all its teachings, encouraging peer groups to love their neighbor (even when their neighbor is their enemy).

6. Benson, *Philosophical Foundations*, 27.

7. Benson, *Philosophical Foundations*, 27.

8. Rickerson, *Building Healthy Families*, 575.

9. Walqui, *Contextual Factors*, 13.

Because learning is affected by community, students need positive and realistic role models within the community to demonstrate the value of learning. It is true that on many levels everyone is a teacher, therefore modeling effects everyone. However, regarding those elevated to be publicly endorsed as teachers, not just anybody should be allowed in such a public position. These teachers/mentors should be a hand-picked group of individuals that provide an example that mirrors and reinforces the intent of those responsible for educating (parents, school, or church officials). The life the professor lives before his students is probably more important than all the lessons he could teach during their schooling. This demonstrates the necessity of the church to be centered on providing role models that demonstrate Christ's joint-love commandment (love God, love neighbor). Therefore, it should become the goal of all Christians to be role models; first, to one another; second, to their immediate neighborhoods; and, finally, to the whole world.

Relationship is what the first and second commandments are all about, and being in community is what relationship is all about. The two (community and relationship) cannot be divorced and maintained separately; they are interdependent. In other words, relationships are not possible outside of social contact. When we are examining any relationship (child/parent, marital, student/student, peers, student/teacher, parishioners, pastor/parishioner, etc.), none of them can be discussed without recognizing both the relationship as a community element and the impact such a community has upon learning.

How Community Empowers Learning

The Power of Community

One of the greatly untapped powers[10] of the church is the power of the church as a biblical community. Whether one is talking about revival or talking about individual growth, community will provide a place for each to thrive. People will develop and growth happens when a church interacts with other people in community. Commitment-based programs are more

---

10. The word "power" that is used throughout this section is not being used in a pejorative sense concerning authority, but rather "power" is being used in the sense that one is given the ability to do something. In this case, the second commandment is what gives people the ability to create a biblical community.

palatable to most people, as compared to other non-community programs. People enjoy the social aspect of community, and the feeling of being at home, when they can sit, talk, and fellowship with people.[11] The feeling of being at home is enjoyed by all (visitors, new converts, youth, children, and even seasoned members of the church).

Christian education is, and should be, the vision and the mission of the church community to all the elements of the community. "Go ye therefore, and teach all nations" (Matt 28:19). As well, Christian educators have a responsibility to join others together and build partnerships that nurture and support the community. "Seeing ye have purified your souls in obeying the truth through the Spirit unto unfeigned love of the brethren, *see that ye* love one another with a pure heart fervently" (1 Pet 1:22). Christian education and community should never be attempted separately, because learning is best when surrounded by a community that provides motivation, support, sympathetic listeners, personal assistance, and, most of all, love for one another. A church, obedient to Christ's command to love their neighbor, creates a community that desires to learn, live, and go to heaven together.

Most human behavior is learned through modeling, imitation, and observation.[12] No greater atmosphere could provide the church with optimum growth than a church unified in Christian community. A Christian learning community provides the catalyst for the togetherness that supports all that the Word of God has instructed the church to become. These learning communities are made up of students, teachers, administrators, leaders, elders, pastors, and counselors working together to experience learning together. Learning is best when the church builds learning communities that integrate education with day-to-day experiences and allow students to see the practical application of knowledge. The lesson of the day is best learned when it can be observed in the life of the believer. This places a tremendous responsibility upon the shoulders of educators. However, "Character and personality of the teacher have a more dominant effect on the lives of the student than the content of the lesson."[13]

Learning communities hold great promise for the church. If the church could only be defined by two terms, they should be *learning* and *community*. When acting in concert together, they greatly enhance one

---

11. Wilhoit and Dettoni, *Nurture*, 59, 204.

12. Lawson, *Historical Foundations*, 27.

13. Downs, *Teaching*, 159.

another. "That their hearts might be comforted, being knit together in love [*community*], and unto all riches of the full assurance of understanding [*learning*], to the acknowledgement of the mystery of God, and of the Father, and of Christ" (Col 2:2).

> *Pastor Levi's frustrations with First Church in general, and Jim and Sharon specifically, were their inability to reach the lost, compounded by an absence of demonstrated love within the church. Many lessons and biblical principles, both preached and modeled, could have, and should have, been modeled across the kitchen table, in the barn, or on a picnic. But Pastor Levi did not demonstrate the behaviors he desired (probably because they had never been demonstrated to him). Maybe they existed, but because there was no learning community in the day-to-day life of the church, no one ever saw them lived out. Jim and Sharon could not live them before each other, or their immediate neighbors, because they had never seen them practically lived out by others.*

The Power of Influence

When one considers the power of influence that is reflected in the human tendency to imitate and assimilate one's surroundings, the power of influence exists to be used and/or abused. Educators identified four classical elements of learning: first, we influence our environment, and our environment influences us; second, we learn through observation; third, our awareness of the consequences of certain behavior influences our choices/learning; and fourth, we are actively, in real time, processing information that is seen and heard.[14]

When considering these four keys in the realm of Christian education, one can extrapolate four equally important elements within the Christian community: first, the church community influences the people of the community, and the people of the community influences the church community; second, there is much to learn about God and his mission/plan by watching the Christian community in which we exist; third, the awareness derived from watching others live with their mistakes and successes has a deterring or heartening affect upon the community; and fourth, the Christian

14. Lawson, *Historical Foundations*, 27.

community should not automatically accept all the visual and audio stimuli without processing it and determining its value for the community.

Consequently, because there is much to learn about God, the church community must be careful how it influences those entrusted to their care and, conversely, be careful what is influencing the church. For example: size, prestige, and finances should not be the sole reason to allow others to influence the church. This is especially true if the influence is void of the joint-love commandment (loving God and loving neighbor). Further, church leadership must understand there is competing influence among the church community and be willing to teach and/or provide correction when needed. Finally, the church must continue to cry out against the immoral influence propagated by much of television, magazines, radio stations, books, and the internet.

The Power of Imitation and Observation

One significant reason that learning is affected by community is that humans are great imitators of their surroundings. "Imitation is the process of adapting to one's surroundings by patching together the beliefs and behaviors of others."[15] This chameleon aspect of humanity is an easily observable trait in all humans, regardless of where they live. Because they have the instinctive ability to imitate, humans adapt in speech, in clothing, in styles, in mannerisms, and in almost every aspect of life. "The concept of observation and imitation has long been an aspect of sound Christian education theory."[16] Imitation need not alarm Christians; however, it is important that we understand that non-discriminative imitation, and the associated influence, can do great harm if ignored. The church community "dare not underestimate the importance of being examples worthy of imitation."[17]

Life in its earliest stages is educated by imitation of its community. Whether a child smiles or frowns a lot is most likely determined by how much his parents smile or frown. Whether a child says "no" or "hallelujah" first is also determined by what he hears his parents say most often. Whether a child grows up to love others or be a racist will also largely depend upon her/his parents. As children grow older, learning comes from imitating the behavior of others and from the rewards and punishments

15. Taylor, *Spiritual Formation*, 94.

16. Downs, *Teaching*, 159.

17. Lawson, *Historical Foundations*, 27.

brought on by imitation. Further reinforcement from imitation comes in three ways: directly watching the model, the consequences (positive or negative) of the observed behavior, and by seeing the affirmation of witnessed behaviors.[18] Throughout the next three sections we will consider the power and influence that is brought into the community by individual groups (parents/caregivers, peers, and mentors.)

The Power of Parents/Caregivers

A major form of influence within a community is found between parents/caregivers and their children. Children assimilate (to hold as one's own) and/or accommodate (to adapt or conform without holding as one's own) the beliefs, desires, habits, patterns, and passions of their parents. Parents and other significant caregivers greatly influence children in their early years, and therefore have a great responsibility to each child for which they care. "If the parents attend church with joy, the children will usually do the same."[19]

"By far the most powerful influence in the lives of children is the approval of their parents."[20] A child's learning is affected by his community of family and friends, and therefore a parent will most often raise a child that is much like him/herself. As children grow older, they continue to need examples, models (such as: parents, youth leaders, teachers, and children's workers), and community rules to help their moral growth. "Listening to other people, hearing their perspectives and integrating them into decisions, helps children and youth learn to think in more mature ways."[21]

The Power of Peers

The Scriptures themselves declare the influence/power between peers within a community, "if one prevail against him, two shall withstand him; and a threefold cord is not quickly broken" (Eccl 4:12). Jesus proclaimed the power of peer community when he instructed the disciples, "For where two or three are gathered together in my name, there am I in the midst of them" (Matt 18:20). Thus, the roles of both the first and second

18. Downs, *Teaching*, 157.
19. Downs, *Teaching*, 149.
20. Downs, *Teaching*, 151.
21. Downs, *Teaching*, 108.

commandments are demonstrated as working together: love for God, coupled with love for neighbor, resulting in the presence of God being enjoined within the community of worshipers.

Another long-term effect of having a peer community is that in later years these same peers have the influence and potential to become effective models for a new generation of peers. When "one generation shall praise [God's] works to another, and . . . declare [his] mighty acts" (Ps 145:4), it will produce repeated generations of increasing size that will praise God. This same principle should be applied to the second commandment; if one generation is obedient to God's Word and love their neighbor, then successive generations will do the same, only better and bigger.

An important spin-off of peer community is the development of life-long friendships. "True fellowship [*community*] goes beyond mere social or recreational activities . . . to building up of one another through expressions of concern, prayer and shared time, utilization of gifts and abilities, and development of warm Christian friendship."[22] Friendship is the result of a peer community that is based upon mutual love and not just a person with whom to pass time. Rather, a friend, according to Proverbs, should be an instrument of learning, "Ointment and perfume rejoice the heart: so doth the sweetness of a man's friend by hearty counsel . . . Iron sharpeneth iron; so a man sharpeneth the countenance of his friend" (Prov 27:9, 17).

The Power of Mentors

Another form of community building, in which imitation/influence is often seen, is provided by mentoring. "Contemporary mentors live out values we hold important and stir us to follow their example."[23] God has always used a man to reach out to others: "How then shall they call on him in whom they have not believed? and how shall they believe in him of whom they have not heard? and how shall they hear without a preacher?" (Rom 10:14). Quoting Howard Hendricks, Joel Comiskey writes, "God always wraps his truth in a person. That's the value of a godly mentor. He shows what biblical truth looks like with skin on it."[24]

Mentoring is not, and should not, be a community experience only utilized by adults. Youth/adolescents in our world, and especially in the

22. Clark et al., *Christian Education*, 398.

23. Comiskey, *Leadership*, 95.

24. Comiskey, *Leadership*, 94.

church, need men and women who will not only be examples, but will also take an interest in them. "[A]dolescents both want and need mirrors [mentors]. Forming spirituality in a teenager is partly a process of showing them mirrors they can trust."[25] Adolescents need models of grace and truth who will also love them unconditionally, teach them how to love their neighbor, and share with them the greatest benefit of the mentoring relationships, someone who will listen. In other words, adolescents need models of grace that will love them as they love themselves.

The Power of a Community Witness

Finally, a discussion of the effect a learning community that loves God and loves neighbors would not be complete unless we considered its impact on the Christian witness. "A united, corporate witness can speak loudly to an unbeliever who joins and observes the congruence between the group's proclamation of the truth and the way members care [love] for one another."[26] Faith and love must exist in the community of believers and be modeled for new converts, wounded/broken humanity, and those being redeemed by the blood of Calvary. Modeling and imitation are powerful means of persistently instilling faith in others. It is equally important to note that second commandment ministry is a biblical setting for modeling and imitation that includes love for even the least. From the birth of a natural child and/or the birth of a spiritual child to the natural death of an elderly person, community and/or loving one's neighbor as oneself indisputably affects their learning. From the cradle to the grave, the Christian community must accept this joint-love commandment (love God, love neighbor) as the learning principle and work on enhancing the community that surrounds them.

The Scriptures Speak on the Role of Christian Education within Community

The Bible clearly focuses on modeling and imitation as part of God's plan for Christian education. "Let your light so shine before men, that they may see your good works, and glorify your Father which is in heaven"

25. Taylor, *Spiritual Formation*, 94.
26. Clark et al., *Christian Education*, 512.

(Matt 5:16). Paul pointed out to the Philippians that they should be imitators of Paul's missionary team because God had given the team to the Philippians as an example. "Brethren, be followers together of me, and mark them which walk so as ye have us for an ensample" (Phil 3:17). Peter warned the leadership of the church of their responsibility to be examples and not lords of the church. "Neither as being lords over God's heritage, but being ensamples to the flock" (1 Pet 5:3).

The purpose for small groups, be it the Christian family or other small groups, is to present themselves as salt and light that models one to another love of neighbor, forgiveness of sins, and eternal mercies. "Ye are the salt of the earth: but if the salt have lost his savor, wherewith shall it be salted? it is thenceforth good for nothing, but to be cast out, and to be trodden under foot of men" (Matt 5:13). Christian education is the salt and light in the world and teaches the love of God in community. To the community of disciples Jesus said, "Let your light so shine before men, that they may see your good works, and glorify your Father which is in heaven" (Matt 5:16).

"Christians should not need to be reminded that good education must involve the body of believers, the church."[27] The entire community of believers must accept its place as educators/followers to a lost and hungry world. Within this community each member is both teacher and follower, and must be a follower of Christ. Paul demonstrated the teacher/follower phenomena to the Corinthians, "Be ye followers of me, even as I also am of Christ" (1 Cor 11:1, 4:16; 2 Thess 3:7). Jesus, too, called the disciples to walk in his footsteps and follow the pattern/example that he had set for them. "For I have given you an example, that ye should do as I have done to you" (John 13:15). As the example of the son following his Father and teaching the disciples, the disciples must also follow the son and teach/make other disciples.

The Second Commandment Establishes the Biblical Model for Christian Education

Human beings are social beings and, because of their strong desire for community, they will look to satisfy this void in their lives when it is absent. As stated before, Boy Scouts, Girl Scouts, clubs, billiard halls, bars, gangs, schools, colleges, the military, and even prisons are all forms of community. Unfortunately, not all community is good community, and

27. Wilhoit and Dettoni, *Nurture*, 59.

the lack of good Christian community will cause people to find community in unhealthy environments. Even in such unhealthy environments, learning is inevitable. There is no way a single pastor can provide enough formal Christian education that it would satisfy the learning needs of everyone. There is therefore a desperate need for the church to develop Christian community, driven by a love for one another, to take up the slack in Christian education through Bible studies, fellowship, social aid, friendship, recreation, and more. Such loving community will provide mentors and examples for others to emulate. The entire Christian community must share in the responsibility, not just the pastor, for the process of forming character, chastening, and nurturing people.

The joint-love commandment (love God, love neighbor) produces an environment where learning is inevitable. Each member of a community that is busy loving her neighbor while loving God will, at the same time, be providing guidance, assistance, understanding, assurance, and a listening ear (each of which is a major element of Christian education). "The community is a discipline of mutual encouragement and mutual testing, keeping me both hopeful and honest about the love that seeks me, the love I seek to be."[28] When this is accomplished within the context of one's neighbor, the Christian community that learns to love their neighbor also learns to love the God who created all. The educational implication for all of us is that within a church all must share a mutual responsibility to love and be loved in the light of God's love. People that participate together in church, dedicated to love for God and others, build a community that cannot soon be defeated.

Where Does the Church Go from Here?

There must be a three-pronged attack if the church is to accept her responsibility as a community of Christian educators. First, an awareness is needed that affirms the public and communal dimensions in the life of the church. We are not the church until we become one body in Christ Jesus. Second, the Christian community must have the support and influence of Christian leaders throughout their faith community. Leaders must be willing to speak out and, at times, correct those who forget that their first obligation while loving God is to love their neighbor. Finally, the church must model, teach, train, and embrace their joint role as ministers/

28. Wilhoit and Dettoni, *Nurture*, 128.

teachers to the next generation. The church must not preach love at church and model hate at home or outside the church. This three-pronged educational attack consists of awareness, support, and training and will bring revival and life to the church. With these three weapons, the church can come out of her huddle with a Bible-based game plan that will provide Christian education within the contexts of biblical community.

Lessons Learned on Christian Education and the Second Commandment

"Your life is the only Bible some will ever read" is an old folk saying with a lot of truth. The apostle Paul said it this way, "Ye are our epistle written in our hearts, known and read of all men" (2 Cor 3:2). This proverb/principle has been around for many years and, in some ways, sums up the significance of what this author has tried to say in this chapter. When the church makes the effort to be a better example and something worthy of imitation, it cannot help but become much better for the effort. "As we encounter [God's] glory reflected in one another, we grasp more of transformation."[29]

Recently, at a small intimate church conference, I had the opportunity to spend time with people in community that I had known for a long time, but only from their public image. In just a few days, the love demonstrated through table fellowship changed everything I thought I understood about them, how I accepted their leadership, and how I understood the message they preached. The visual witness of practical love for God and neighbor was more valuable to this writer than the twelve years of post-graduate studies. "Good lectures and powerful preaching may be stimuli for significant education, but . . . [this story] reminds us that people must interact with each other in order to grow."[30]

This author believes that community affects every learning environment, but especially the environment of Christian education. While no element of learning goes untouched by the positive influence of community, the Bible's call to both community and Christian education is loud and clear. Learning must not be separated solely into isolated and lonely lecture halls; rather, they should be experienced together within the warm bosom of the second commandment and a church committed to community. When one sees love in action, feels the love for themselves,

29. Wilhoit and Dettoni, *Nurture*, 241.
30. Wilhoit and Dettoni, *Nurture*, 59.

and is encouraged to love others, a strong bond is created that will with-stand even the fiercest of storms.

> *Pastor Levi had hoped that Jim, Sharon, and other members of First Church would learn Christian principles by just coming to church and sitting on the pews. It was easy for him to cast the blame on his church as being lazy and/or unmotivated. However, even if Pastor Levi was working twenty hours each day and leading an exemplary life, much of it was wasted (as an example) because there was no one present to imitate the role model he set forth (besides his own family). Without exposure to the working of the church community, no one knew what was expected of them. Consequently, the lack of fellowship among church members (and pastor) blocked the educational attempts of Pastor Levi, blocked Jim and Sharon's example to their neighbors, blocked Jim's witness to Betty on the job, and blocked the church's efforts to reach out to their community.*

8

The Second Commandment
in Christian Counseling

Where no counsel is, the people fall: but in the multitude of
counsellors there is safety . . . Without counsel purposes are
disappointed: but in the multitude of counsellors they are
established.

—PROV 11:14; 15:22

*Lonely and stumbling through life, Mary lived through each week
(Mary was the mother that lived in the run-down house on the other
side of Jim and Sharon). If only she could make it until Monday at
three o'clock in the afternoon. Then, once again, she could see her
psychiatrist. Oh, how wonderful it was to have someone to talk
with besides her drunk husband and screaming kids; someone who
would listen and not judge; someone who would pay attention to
her problems; and someone who could provide some direction! But
this was Friday afternoon at four o'clock, and she still had to make it
through two days and twenty-three hours; three long nights of loneliness, tears, and sadness. Week after week, the only highlight of her
long week was the visit to the community's mental health offices. She
lived for that hour each week when she could have the counselor all
to herself. She understood that he was busy and could only spare an
hour, but what was she to do the rest of the week and all through the
nights? She had been seeing him for the better part of a year, trying
to deal with her long, empty life of loneliness. What was she going to
do? Suicide sometimes seemed almost attractive!*

> *Mary often watched the next-door neighbors, Jim and Sharon, leave for church and wondered what they had to be so happy about. Of course, they had jobs, money, friends, and a church that seemed to care! But where was her community? Who would fill the gap in her emotional vacuum? Unfortunately for Mary, Jim and Sharon were also lonely and did not understand the value of second commandment ministry. Their lack of godly love for each other was amplified in relationships outside their marriage. Further, neither Jim nor Sharon understood that much of the counseling vacuum in Mary's life could be filled by ordinary people dedicated to the joint-love commandment given by Jesus (love God and love neighbor). So, three lonely people lived side by side; two lonely people went to church while the other stayed home. The solution for all three can be found in the following words, "Surely much of the answer is found in the role of the church as a community of believers who are dedicated to encouraging and building up one another."[1]*

As illustrated above, Christian counseling is not something that is done successfully in a vacuum (by itself without the backing of a church community). Rather, the counselee must be supported by a large network that includes, but is not limited to, spouse, friends, co-workers, family, neighbors, volunteers, pastors, churches, and more. All these elements make up the counselee's community, and this community is important to the well-being of the counselee.[2] This collaborative approach will determine the success of any counseling enterprise that the church undertakes. Just as the medical field has found greater success in the field of physical healing when a holistic approach is used (doctor, nurse, aide, social worker, chaplain, etc.), so also will the counseling field find greater success in a collaborative approach. The counseling field often "does not see the whole picture. I am tired of reading books on Christian counseling that give just one side of the issue and suggest that problems can be resolved by applying one special technique . . . God wants to restore his image in us: not in part of us but in the whole."[3]

After considering the church's obligation to loving their neighbor and the resulting community in previous chapters, let us consider in this chapter

1. Collins, *Biblical Basis*, 203–8.
2. Benner, *Strategic Pastoral Counseling*, 49–50.
3. Hughes, *Every Day Light*, 233.

the church's counseling role in a community built upon the second commandment. Second, the church must consider why this counseling role is so important in today's world. Third, the counseling role of today's church is supported by a firm biblical foundation. Finally, the church needs to develop precise ways to provide/promote community in the life of the counselee and counseling in the life of the larger community.

There is no way a single pastor of any given church can provide pastoral care and/or counseling around the clock for those in need of assistance. There is a desperate need for the whole church to develop Christian community through obedience to the joint-love commandment (love God and love neighbor) (as explained in chapter 6 under the subtitle, *Who Provides Pastoral Care? Priesthood of All Believers*). This community must be one that exists as a collective, where all believers care for all! When all believers that love God and neighbor use their individual giftings to care for all, the overwhelming need of the church will be better satisfied and can provide a better approach to people's problems. Some researchers believe that such a community can back up, and may in many cases replace, the need for individual counseling.[4]

Let the Scriptures Speak for Community-Based Counseling

The idea of community being one of the counseling tools of the church, and quite possibly the tool we now call pastoral counseling, can be dated back to the Old Testament. Consider the power of community demonstrated in the following verse in Isaiah that encouraged Israel by informing them that their island enemies would fear them and their God if they would practice community.

> The isles saw *it*, and feared; the ends of the earth were afraid, drew near, and came. They helped every one his neighbor; and every one said to his brother, Be of good courage. So the carpenter encouraged the goldsmith, *and* he that smootheth *with* the hammer him that smote the anvil, saying, It *is* ready for the soldering: and he fastened it with nails, *that* it should not be moved (Isa 41:5–7).

Paul understood the power of community when he told the Galatians, "Bear ye one another's burdens, and so fulfill the law of Christ" (Gal 6:2). "When we are in the habit of 'bearing one another's burden' and

---

4. Collins, *Biblical Basis*, 132.

casting our burdens on God in prayer, then we are better prepared for facing illness and death when they come."[5]

From the early days, the church found strength in community, "And they continued steadfastly in the apostles' doctrine and fellowship, and in breaking of bread, and in prayers" (Acts 2:42). A principle outlined in the New Testament (and covered in previous chapters) is that people imitate and follow people, "If there be therefore any consolation in Christ, if any comfort of love, if any fellowship of the Spirit, if any bowels and mercies, fulfill ye my joy, that ye be likeminded, having the same love, being of one accord, of one mind" (Phil 2:1–2). Early Christians were taught, in response to the second commandment given by Christ, that community was a part of being in God's family, and division or lack of community was antichrist. Comfort was found in sharing with one's community, and pain in the body was experienced by the whole. "That there should be no schism in the body; but that the members should have the same care one for another. And whether one member suffer, all the members suffer with it; or one member be honored, all the members rejoice with it" (1 Cor 12:25–26).

Practical community was intended by Christ to be more than just a prayer or thought on behalf of our fellow Christians. "If a brother or sister be naked, and destitute of daily food, And one of you say unto them, Depart in peace, be ye warmed and filled; notwithstanding ye give them not those things which are needful to the body; what doth it profit?" (Jas 2:15–16). Rather, we are instructed, "Let every one of us please his neighbor for his good to edification" (Rom 15:2). The church needs to build practical community today based upon the first and second commandments; first, to our neighbors sitting next to us on the pew; second, to our next-door neighbors; and, finally, to our neighbors around the world.

We have for too long *just* prayed and *just* fasted for the hurting among us. It is high time that, when we get off our knees, we become part of the lives of our neighbors, being the community that they need, and filling the gaps that exist in every church. However, such community is not possible unless Christians are unwaveringly committed to loving God and loving one's neighbor. We have heard for years that many new converts just slipped through the gap. The gaps exist because the church is not being the community that is needed. Our newly converted neighbors need more than our prayers and our money; they need our time, our ears, our shoulders, and our desire to please and edify. In other words,

---

5. Collins, *Biblical Basis*, 342.

someone who will reach into the fire, while hating the very garments spotted by the flesh, having compassion, pulling them from the fire, and making a difference (Jude 1:21–23).

The church today lives in a very busy world, and everyone seems to use the excuse of how little time there is. However, let the whole church consider its purpose, "Even for this same purpose have I raised thee up, that I might show my power in thee, and that my name might be declared throughout all the earth" (Rom 9:17). Our goals and priorities must be to address the need for God's power and name within our community, with the same love, sensitivity, and skill of Christ.[6] No one had a greater or more important agenda than Christ, yet John reminds us, "Greater love hath no man than this, that a man lay down his life for his friends" (John 15:13).

Conclusively, the Scriptures compel us to build a community and thus "be there" for our neighbor. "If any *man* will come after [Jesus], let him deny himself, and take up his cross, and follow [Jesus]" (Matt 16:24). One may ask, "What did the church do for almost two thousand years without the psychological counseling movement?" Lynda Doty, in her book, *Apostolic Counseling; Helping God's People God's Way,* answers that question: it was the community of believers that encouraged, strengthened, ministered, and guided one another through the problems of their day.[7]

Community and Counseling

How can the church respond to the overwhelming mental and emotional illnesses that have flooded the world, overcome with loneliness and suicide? In times past, when religion placed people into community groups, they were "less lonely and isolated . . . less inclined to get depressed or to attempt suicide."[8] Churches must once again become the kind of communities where people feel loved, welcomed, wanted, and accepted. Such pastoral communities, infused with their love for God and their love for their neighbors, can provide hope in a hopeless world that is rapidly spinning out of control. "Much more helpful is the support that comes from a community that says, 'We are with you in this pain and are praying for you, even though we don't completely understand it.'"[9]

6. Barna, *Growing True Disciples*, 22-23.

7. Doty, *Apostolic Counseling*, 144.

8. Collins, *Biblical Basis*, 117.

9. Collins, *Biblical Basis*, 117.

Unfortunately, at least in North America, the church has absorbed the individualistic nature of its culture, moved away from being a place that integrates people into the group, and has become a place where strangers sit and listen to a religious lecture. Pastors must quit seeing themselves as the men/women with all the answers and step up to a larger, more biblical, responsibility of the second commandment. The first responsibility of the pastoral counselor should be to link up the hurting with a church community that can provide the support and love that is necessary for long-term health.[10] When people in community view how others deal with problems, difficulties, and disappointments, their own situation does not seem as foreboding or impossible.

Jay E. Adams used the idea of pastoral counselors utilizing clients as "client counselors" or assistant counselors.[11] This—"all helping all" idea—can carry one another's burdens from day to day and prevent relapses between sessions. If churches are to grow beyond the size which the single pastor can handle, pastors must begin to see themselves as facilitators of resources rather than the Bible-answer man/woman. The day has come when all men and women of the Spirit must step up and make themselves available to be used by the Spirit. Those who are spiritual (defined as one who has the Spirit), have for too long passed off the church's biblical responsibility to restore their brother/sister, when taken in a fault (Gal 6:1). Because the church has failed to see the responsibility for all the people to become the people of God, the church has passed care off to professionals (counselors, psychiatrists, marital therapists, social workers, etc.). However, the Scriptures compel the church, with the Spirit, to restore the fallen one in meekness, remembering that it may be ourselves next who need restoration.

Community and Personal Issues

We are living in a selfish world—maybe the worst ever since the beginning of time. The world around us, especially in America, has become a place "all about me!" It should come as no surprise that the psychiatric field has for many years been among the fastest-growing job fields in Western civilization, due to the rise of depression, loneliness, and mental illness. However, "in contrast [to self-centeredness], when there is a willing attempt to help others, including depressed people, then everybody benefits,

10. Benner, *Strategic Pastoral Counseling*, 27.
11. Adams, *Competent to Counsel*, 241.

and depression may be reduced."[12] Once again, we see that the creation of a caring community in love with their neighbors is an indirect way to prevent depression, mental illness, suicide, and so many other issues. It is other-centeredness (a concern for others) that must replace self-centeredness when the church becomes a part of the community of believers in obedience to the joint-love commandment.

A feeling of isolation (and certainly the fact of isolation) breeds anger, loneliness, and violence in America. Repeated violence has been attributed to Americans being isolated from society. However, when people are part of a whole, they feel more compelled to conform to the whole through others' examples, the disapproval of the community, and the threat of isolation. "In the home, but also in the church and school, people can be taught by words and example to evaluate each anger-arousing situation."[13] Interestingly, the Yupik (an Alaskan native people living on the Bering Sea) justice system, prior to the encroachment of Western civilization, used varying degrees of isolation to punish people for crimes committed. Equally interesting was the lack of crime; for the most part, crime came with Western civilization. The Yupik, as well as all men, learned to control the tendency of man to do evil by the influence exercised by the community in which they lived. For all of time, the less community influence, the greater the evil, crime, and violence in the world.

Community and Developmental Issues

There seems to have been more written on the family community and their influence upon developmental issues than any other subject. This may be true because community (or the lack of community) and its influences upon development are easier to see, understand, and explain within the context of the family than in any other context. Collins wrote, "Modeling, as we have noted, is one of the most important means of teaching adolescents."[14] The concept, *Johnnie is just like his daddy*, is not only easy to see, but oftentimes humorous.

While imitation may be humorous at times, the rise in crime, pregnancy, and suicide among teens makes it a very serious problem. The rising problems emphasize the failure of America's parents to provide an example

12. Collins, *Biblical Basis*, 117.

13. Collins, *Biblical Basis*, 132.

14. Collins, *Biblical Basis*, 180.

to the next generation. However, there is hope/help: "Parents can be helped to be example believers."[15] If the children are to be helped, the parents must first be helped; and it is the church, as the community of believers, that must be primed and ready to provide the community help needed. If we are to help this generation's children, the faith and help exhibited, by both the church and the parents, must be more than just an idle commitment, but must be demonstrated by a commitment to loving God and loving one's neighbor—often that neighbor is those of our own household. "They [adolescents] are much more impressed when their parents show that theirs is a vital faith, characterized by a sincere commitment to Jesus Christ and a daily willingness to worship and serve him."[16]

Community and Interpersonal Issues

The modern use of terminology indicating close relationships, such as *best friends, buddies,* and *Facebook friends,* has been demeaned to the point where it seems to mean less than *acquaintances* did just a few years ago. "Some counselees have rarely experienced mutual respect or good relationships with another human being."[17] It is a blight upon a society when some people only see a counselor to help them meet new friends. This is not to say that they should not be helped, but just the fact that they need help making friends sheds the light on an uncomfortable trend of society. Learning to make friends was what kindergarten was all about fifty years ago. This author can remember children being held back because they had not accomplished this very simple task by the end of their kindergarten school year. Thankfully, the loneliness, and/or lack of interpersonal relationships from which many people suffer, is exactly the kind of problem that a genuine love for neighbor can eliminate.

Radical love for one's neighbors was one of the reasons for the phenomenal growth in the New Testament. It was not signs or wonders only, but rather it was the awe of the church's community for which that society was so desperately seeking. A large portion of the epistles was dedicated to either encourage interpersonal relationships (community) or eliminate the pitfalls that would destroy the same. If the New Testament community is to live on today, the church must create a safe atmosphere where

---

15. Collins, *Biblical Basis,* 163.

16. Collins, *Biblical Basis,* 178.

17. Collins, *Biblical Basis,* 238.

people can openly talk about personal strengths and weaknesses with others within the community.

In other words, Christians must develop interpersonal relationships (friends, brothers, sisters, mentors, prayer partners, accountability partners, and more) with their new family in Christ. Transformation and change are the very nature of Christian conversion where one is motivated by sharing, knowing, caring, and growing in mutual community. There is a close relationship between building true friendships (the second commandment) and building one's relationship with God (the first commandment). The church must be a community of relationships where both our love for God and our love for our neighbor is paramount.

Community and Identity Issues

Low self-esteem seems to be the catchword of this generation, and it has become the excuse for a wide variety of mental illnesses and violent crimes. Once again, however, "Being accepted by a group of people can do much to stimulate self-esteem and help an individual feel worthwhile."[18] Let the church not sit idly by loving God while the world goes to hell, and say that there is nothing that she can do. Rather, let the church be a community of people committed to loving, encouraging, valuing, and promoting self-esteem; having compassion, making a difference, and saving others bound with fear, "pulling them out of the fire; hating even the garment spotted by the flesh" (Jude 1:22–23). The hope found in a true community of believers, committed to loving their neighbors, is just as strong today as it was in the days following Pentecost, when thousands were filled with God's Spirit.

It is sometimes amazing how quickly the medical profession will turn to medication to elevate one's feelings of worth (self-esteem), when it is well documented that "an active involvement in a church or other religious group can also boost self-esteem."[19] There is nothing that assists in eliminating low self-esteem like personal relationships, especially when they are true relationships based upon the biblical joint-love commandment. It may be true that the world is a more stressful place in which to live than it was years ago; therefore, one's feelings are worn down until one's self-esteem is damaged, and a feeling of inferiority persists. Nevertheless, the burden

18. Collins, *Biblical Basis*, 323.
19. Collins, *Biblical Basis*, 323.

is lightened, and problems are prevented, when friends and fellow church members provide loving support and encouragement.

The two-thousand-year-old New Testament commitment to a community that follows the teaching of Jesus remains the answer for identity issues. "The first of all the commandments is, Hear, O Israel; The Lord our God is one Lord: And thou shalt love the Lord thy God with all thy heart, and with all thy soul, and with all thy mind, and with all thy strength: this is the first commandment. And the second is like, namely this, Thou shalt love thy neighbour as thyself. There is none other commandment greater than these" (Mark 12:29–31).

Community and Family Issues

Unfortunately, a church without a love for her neighbors has become a non-reproducing body that is unable to affect day-to-day relationships. However, this was not, and is not, God's plan. God himself instituted community when he designed the first garden over six thousand years ago. Quickly God realized that it was not good for man to be alone, so he made him a companion (Gen 2:18). From the beginning of time, the human family provided help and guidance to one another. Strong family units are often the backbone of the church community. Because of that, when "working together, families in the church can help other families and individuals meet crises and cope with the realities of life."[20]

The inter-weaving of families within a community has immense value in a time of trouble, grief, sorrow, and death. "Frequently the family members are helped by neighbors, friends, coworkers, and fellow church members. Professionals refer to this network of relatives and friends as a support system."[21] Having stood by the bedside of dozens of dying parishioners and hundreds of hospice patients, this author can speak with authority; there is no sadder situation than seeing someone having to die or be sick alone. There is no time in which the community of believers has a greater value than in such times of trouble. The ongoing support provided by the presence of a well-connected church community soothes the miles walked while working through problems, living with grief, and struggling with loss.

If the church is to stabilize and save the families within the community of believers, it must first strengthen and stabilize the marriages within

20. Collins, *Biblical Basis*, 446.

21. Collins, *Biblical Basis*, 445.

the community. While stating that community cannot take the place of marriage counseling, one cannot deny that community has a significant part in the success or failure of one's marriage. "[Marriage] counseling, with few exceptions, is a second-best operation."[22] Charles Stewart goes on to say that the best approach for saving marriages is when a community of believers think out and plan a preemptive family life education program that will help couples and families grow together as Christians. The local church must be the place where families can find help for their marriages, their children, and all manner of familial/generational issues.

> Jim and Sharon's marriage would have, and may still, benefit from such community. They, like most Americans, are marrying without any consideration as to the community that they are supposed to create by their union. Further, they had given no thought as to the larger community of which their marriage should be an integral part. Pastor Levi, if he had been involved in second commandment ministry, would have modeled to them marital community by being in fellowship with them on a regular basis. Further, if Pastor Levi had been in fellowship with Jim and Sharon, he would not have been so shocked by the announcement of their marital demise. As well, there would have undoubtedly been countless opportunities to talk with them about their problems, and such informal counseling sessions (done in a community setting) may have prevented the acceleration of marital difficulties.

Community and Other Issues

There remains a multitude of issues from which one could produce examples with which to support an active role of a Bible-based community in people's lives. From this vast list, consider one more important issue. Missing from many of America's churches is the growing number of mentally handicapped people in our cities. However, these people are just as much in need of the real community found in the second commandment as anyone else. Oftentimes they have just as much to offer the community as the next

22. Stewart, *Minister*, 190.

person. "[T]he local body of believers must be at the center of supportive care for those with mentally incapacitated family members."[23]

Because of one church's willingness to accept the mentally handicapped, they have had a steady stream of them through their church, some attending for many years. One young man always had a smile and a word of encouragement for everyone (that is, if you stopped long enough to understand what he was saying). His mother had been in the church her whole life, but she had bounced to every church in the area because she could not find a place that would accept her son. He was thirty-six years old when he came to the church this author pastored, had spent his whole life on church pews, and had never been baptized, even though he asked almost every week for someone to baptize him. He wanted to, "Swim, just like everyone else, so [he] could go to heaven too!" One of the greatest thrills of this author's life was to baptize him into the body of Christ. It was so sad that many pastors had forbade it, simply because they felt "he did not fully understand." However, he understood that he needed to be baptized in obedience to the Scriptures, and that was good enough for this pastor. "The community, and especially the church, can provide the ongoing support, warmth, acceptance, caring, and contact with reality [for people with mental disorders] that busy professionals often have limited time to give."[24]

Lessons Learned from Counseling, Community, and the Second Commandment

For too many years the implications of the second commandment within the church have been ignored, or at the very least not appreciated, by the church. Consequently, community has been absent, or at least not encouraged, alongside of pastoral counseling. While it is not the intention to eliminate or minimize those qualified to provide pastoral or clinical counseling, it is, however, the intention to send a loud and clear cry to the church to wake out of sleep and become a community that loves their neighbor (as well, love their God), build a community within which community can thrive, and invite the world to become part of that community. The church must assume its responsibility as a community of believers, provide lay pastoral care training, and begin utilizing those trained to assist in restoring troubled people to fully productive lives. One thing is certain, no one (and

23. Collins, *Biblical Basis*, 482.
24. Collins, *Biblical Basis*, 481.

not even any two) can build community in the way Christ desires believers to build. "God's design and plan is that every Christian be a functioning body of Christ; that every Christian contribute to the process."[25]

A community of believers, when it exists in harmony with both the first (loving God) and second (loving neighbor) commandments, is the mighty fortress of our God, the very body of Christ (1 Cor 12:27). Therefore, this community, as the body of Christ, possesses great power and strength. The massive number of caribou, that roam through Alaska in herds, range from eighty thousand to one hundred fifty thousand animals. US Fish and Game claims that a healthy herd of caribou must have between fifty thousand and eighty thousand animals. This is because they cannot survive without immense community support. A child with a knife can kill an isolated caribou, but, within a herd of thousands, it is difficult for the mighty timber wolf to take down and kill one. The church is like that; alone, the isolated Christian is vulnerable to the slightest provocation, but collectively, God's truth marches on through fire, famine, and flood. Church members that become isolated in their own little worlds of loneliness are finding their lives shattered. Isolated counseling is often not enough, but together with a community of believers that is built on a foundation of the joint-love commandments, broken church members can find the daily joy and happiness necessary to face their tomorrows.

"From the time of its beginning, the body of Christ, the church, has been a helping community . . . [they] have demonstrated . . . healing, sustaining, guiding, and mending broken interpersonal relationships."[26] Unfortunately, in many places community has died because of a lack of faithfulness to the second commandment. In their place, the church has become little more than a status symbol or a social club that excludes, rather than loves, the undesirables, the disenfranchised, and the time consumers. The streets and homes of America are filled with lonely people looking for answers, looking for someone to care. In closing this chapter, I am compelled to ask the question: Shouldn't that caring come from my church?

25. Getz, *Building*, 110.
26. Collins, *Biblical Basis*, 144.

9

The Second Commandment
at the Time of Death

So when this corruptible shall have put on incorruption, and this mortal shall have put on immortality, then shall be brought to pass the saying that is written, Death is swallowed up in victory. O death, where is thy sting? O grave, where is thy victory? The sting of death is sin; and the strength of sin is the law. But thanks be to God, which giveth us the victory through our Lord Jesus Christ.

—1 COR 15:54–57

The phone rang and the voice on the other end was a nurse at the hospital, "Fred is dying, and the family is asking for Pastor Levi to come!" Once again, Pastor Levi sank to his knees beside the phone and cried out to God in anguish, "What am I supposed to do? What am I supposed to say?" As pastor, he hated the death bed more than anything else. Yet somehow, he immediately knew that the command to love the least of his neighbors would—should—must extend to the injured, the sick, the afflicted, and the dying. As he prayed, he remembered a blog that he had seen some time back and scrambled to find the link (deathministry.blogspot.com; dated Sept. 23, 2014):

I paused outside the room to gather my thoughts and breathe a prayer for the job that was ahead.[1] The hospice nurse had called and informed me of a new patient that had a fast-growing cancer on her face, neck, and head. She was not expected to live very long. A month ago, she had seemed healthy, living independently, and had no visible symptoms. The nurse had tried to prepare me for a rather unsightly situation and the considerable difficulty in controlling the pain.

On entering the room, darkened because of the closed drapes and dimmed lights, my eyes slowly adjusted to the darkness. Writhing in pain on the bed was a terribly disfigured woman with multiple, open, weeping tumors on her head, of which one seemed as large as a softball; dozens of other tumors ranged in size from a marble to a golf ball. Significant amounts of morphine had been administered but had little effect on her pain. Her chart said that she was not a practicing Christian but had expressed a desire to see the chaplain upon admission (some days ago, prior to being on hospice). She is elderly, but her body seems to be rather healthy, compared to her head. She has a decreased level of consciousness (due to medication and disease) and is alert only to herself, her pain, and her end-of-life concerns.

Kim was every bit as bad as can be imagined. She tossed and turned on her bed; her skin was moist and clammy; the sores on her head were gruesome; and the smell was almost unbearable. I pushed up the chair as close to the bed as it would go and sat down. When I took her hand, I could feel the grip tighten around mine (somewhere inside she was still reaching out for community). She whispered a word (one of the two words she said while I was there) to me before I could say anything: "Scared!" I told her who I was and did not receive any response other than her hand tightly gripping mine. Her collar-length hair was matted, wet, and hanging in her face. I reached out my other hand and began moving the hair out of her face and running my fingers through her hair and over the tumors that were claiming her life. Her response was

---

1. This is an actual day in the life of a hospice chaplain written by this author in 2014. Changes in names, situations, and demographics have been made to protect the anonymity, privacy, and dignity of the patients and their families.

almost immediate as she calmed down and began to fall more comfortably asleep. The nurse came in and said, "Thank God you're here. We haven't been able to do anything for her." Amazing what a touch can do when time is given, and the effort is made! Over the next few hours, I said my prayer, even told the story of how Jesus touched the leper, played some hymns on my iPod, but mostly just held her hand and touched her head and hair.

An hour later her arm relaxed as her coma deepened, and I was able to go. The pager on my phone beeped as I walked down the hall, troubled once again over my last visit. Now the phone was beeping again, a beep that I had learned to associate with a crisis. A beep that pulled me from my troubled reflections, Was I doing enough? Were the songs/ Scriptures/prayers meaningful? Had I briefly been able to highlight the joined hands of God and man?

The text message read, "New patient in Freemont, may die at any moment. Can you come today and do intake/assessment?" A few phone calls later, I had rearranged my schedule, postponed less critical appointments, picked up a lunch for the one hundred sixty-mile, round-trip journey, and headed down the road in my car to a new, unknown crisis. Would I be able to provide comfort? Could I extend the hand of Christ to care for the sick, diseased, and/or demented?

While I drove out to the house, I received a call from the hospice social worker with a briefing on what was known. The patient was an elderly woman with an inoperable cranial aneurism that could burst at any time. As well, she had an implanted pacemaker/defibrillator that kept firing irregularly whenever the heart failed to fire on its own. She had several children of varying involvement. Finally, she also had some form of dementia.

When I arrived at the house, the front door was ajar, so I walked on in (a practice most deemed appropriate/safe in rural areas) and found the family room crowded with family and hospice workers trying to provide initial services to the family and client. As is often the case, other than a precursory greeting and/or examination, the demented patient was being ignored, and the attention was being given to the family. It is the chaplain's job to "spend time" with the patient. I knelt next to the wheelchair and put my arm on the back of the chair. The patient immediately gave me a sloppy hug and laid her head on my shoulder. She welcomed me warmly and denied any pain. We talked of her family, of whom she could provide little information regarding the number or names of her children. She did not know the day, month, or year. She was unable to tell where she was, other than "Home!"

Finally, I asked the questions I am forced to ask, for her records, about her faith tradition. She immediately stated that she was Catholic. When asked if she had always been Catholic, she stated, "No! I just changed a few weeks ago!" A family member in the background stated, "More like fifty years ago!" When asked what she was before she became Catholic (seeing that it felt so fresh and recent to her), she again answered quickly, stating that she grew up Mormon. When asked if she thought of herself as either Catholic or Mormon, she stated that she wasn't sure. When asked if I could contact a Catholic priest or Mormon elder for her, she said, "No! The first one didn't approve of my first marriage [to a Catholic man], and the second didn't approve of my divorce and second marriage. Besides, my new husband is United Church of Christ!" When asked if she ever went to church with her husband, she again informed me, "He doesn't go to his church either, because they didn't approve of me!" She then, without prompting, dropped a bombshell on me, "Besides, we have you now [giving me a little, slobbery hug and kiss on the cheek]. You will be our pastor now!" When I asked her husband if I could contact someone for him, to act as a spiritual advisor, he too affirmed his wife's words, "No, we have not attended church in forty years, and I am sure that you can take care of any religious needs we have." It is worth noting here that while she could not remember the names of her children, she could quite accurately relate the painful history of a rather fractured faith background.

What do I do for these ladies? What can I offer them? What does the ecclesia/church have to offer them? How can the gospel be presented to them this late in the situation? What form would the kerygma (spoken word) take, and what should it look like? In this context I do not stand at a podium, take a text, and pontificate about some aspect of the scripture, a format that anticipates an allotment of time in which to reflect, incorporate, and by which to become empowered. On the other hand, my actions become the *kerygma* for the patient, and therefore, my life/actions, as the lived sermon, must be a major consideration of what is to be done when ministering to people at the time of death.

No PASTORAL CARE DUTY of the church is more difficult, more unpleasant, and potentially more important than the care provided at the time of death. Because of these reasons, pastoral care at the time of death is often postponed, or avoided completely, by the pastor/church. In this chapter we will first consider the beauty of loving (and being loved) in the most undesirable situations as an alternative view of caring at the time of death. Second, we will demonstrate how the early (first and second century) church found beauty in living the second commandment teachings of Jesus (see chapters 2–4), specifically at the time of death. Third, we will create a practical model of care for use at the time of death that is influenced by the joint-love commandment (love for God and neighbor).

Finding Beauty in the Second Commandment at the Time of Death

Mystery seems to envelope the subject of beauty. Why do some see or find beauty in difficult situations and others seem unable to comprehend the beauty? Why do some look beyond the grief and see the love that is present in such grief? This same sense of mystery occurs when providing care and accompanying the patient at the time of death. A spirituality that evokes something holy (the presence of God in the lowest of valleys) can only be described as a place of beauty. Such beauty can only be recognized as God's, and beckons to those that accompany the patient to the very gates of the other side. The demise of beauty at the time of death is often the result of the loss of awareness for God and his beauty and distraction caused by grief, pain, and suffering.

It would be difficult, if not impossible, to attempt to define and understand beauty without considering the work of Jonathan Edwards, who is the most prolific writer on beauty, with beauty being "central and more pervasive [*in his writings*] than in any other text in the history of Christian theology." Jonathan Edwards was an eighteenth-century theologian who believed that the theology of beauty "begins and ends with God . . . an extraordinary vision of the divine Beauty replicating itself in all of creation."[2] Further, Edwards felt it was not enough just to *know* the definition of beauty in some logical format; "instead, one had to have a *sense* of it or, we might say, one had to *experience* God's beauty for oneself."[3] It is just such a *sense* of beauty that can be found in the presence of a Holy God at the time of death. "[One] does not merely rationally believe that God is glorious, but he has a sense of the gloriousness of God in his heart."[4]

Therefore, like the psalmist, there is one thing that I desire in all that I do, and the one thing that I will seek after, is to behold the beauty of the Lord (Ps 27:4)! I contend that it is therefore the church's job at the time of death to provide the vehicle, trigger the aura, or hold up the mirror that allows/helps the dying and their families to find a place of beauty through the actions of God's people. Pastors, churches, volunteers, musicians, etc. give this "beauty away so that the rest of the world may, in the midst of squalor, ugliness, and pain, remember that beauty is possible."[5]

The Scriptures present God's beauty: "behold the beauty of the Lord" (Ps 27:4); the very being of God testifies to his beauty. God is beauty! God's beauty is also associated with his moral character; God's excellence, honor, and majesty exude his beauty throughout all of creation, especially humanity created in his image (Gen 1:26). "Out of Zion, the perfection of beauty, God hath shined" (Ps 50:2). Throughout Scripture there is no greater moral virtue coupled with beauty than God's holiness. The psalmist David exhorted God's creation to worship the Lord in the beauty of holiness and declared that God would live among those who worshiped him in such beauty (Ps 29:2; 22:3). The final idea associating God with beauty is his continued work in creation. Beautiful, because the beauty of the Lord our God is upon his creation and has established that his ongoing work is now in the hands of his creation (Ps 90:17). Forever, oh God, you are beauty; your creation, created in your image, is beauty; and your beauty continues in the work of your creation.

2. Lane, *Ravished by Beauty*, 171–72.

3. Moore, *Hope of Beauty*, 161.

4. Lane, *Ravished by Beauty*, 184.

5. O'Donohue, *Beauty*, 215.

Creation is drawn to God's beauty and the church should be concerned with living in the presence of such beauty more than anything else. Maybe we should not be as concerned with finding new beauty, but in recognizing God's existing beauty and the ongoing work of beauty by his creative work, which surrounds creation every day. However, lifting appealing notions of the beauty of God and God's world is not a complete picture. To explore notions of beauty at the time of death, we must acknowledge the realities of the ugliness that permeates the world. If God is beauty, if he exudes beauty in his ongoing creation, and if his creation participates in this beauty, where is this beauty when the sometimes-horrific realities of life are present? When comparing the suffering in our world up against God's beauty, it seems difficult to see because it is often overlooked, ignored, or clouded by the distractions of disease, pain, and other end-of-life issues.

Because of the decline in celebration and worship of God's beauty, it is possible that God's being is ignored and his beauty is hidden. Many do not take God seriously or pay close attention to things associated with God, his work, and his church. God is still trying to make his being "known through the things of this world, and he lamented the fact that people seem so dull of hearing and blind to the beauty and glory that God is revealing all around them."[6] Therefore, many simply do not take the time to know his beauty, and therefore do not anticipate its existence in life or in death.

A "persistent longing for beauty can serve as a starting point" or a place of awakening "a true sense of beauty in this age of ugliness and death."[7] The call today is to let God take his rightful place in one's world, and when one does, one becomes more aware of his beauty in the world. "When we waken to beauty, we keep desire alive in its freshness, passion, and creativity. Beauty is not a deadener but a quickener!"[8] As one awakens in her approach to God, she enters the presence of One who is the embodiment of all things beautiful. Being aware in God's presence provides space for holy moments of beauty, "How great is his goodness, and how great is his beauty" (Zech 9:17)!

The point of this section is to call the church to awaken to the beauty in God's creation and to the beauty in the lives of his creation. The mentally and physically exhausting work at the time of death is especially suited for seeing God's beauty; "Precious in the sight of the Lord is the death of his

6. Hopkins, *Poems and Prose*, 166.

7. Moore, *Hope of Beauty*, 158.

8. O'Donohue, *Beauty*, 4.

saints" (Ps 116:15). Like a candle shining in a dark room, the suffering and pain experienced in the beauty of the cross is an example of how God's beauty can shine in such horrific situations. Unfortunately, most of those that are dying, rarely, if ever, knew God in his beauty; therefore "it makes sense for us to believe that, if there is to be any recovery of beauty in this age of ugliness and death, it must arise from within the community of those who know God today."[9] The church at the bedside of the dying must become the mirror in which both patients and their families can see God's beauty in their lives and the world around them. The mirror triggers the aura of times past, when God's beauty had been especially present to them, and provides a space for beauty to be appreciated again.

There was no limit to which God would go to right the full brokenness of creation, that it might be in harmony with his beauty; the ugliness of the cross was the boldest symbol of beauty in all history. The church (be they pastor or volunteer) must hold up a mirror, so the world can see its own inherent beauty as one created by God. When one recognizes the beauty of God throughout life, one can join with the rest of humanity that bends toward the existence of God's eternal beauty. When one sees this beauty, there is a sense of homecoming, a sense of belonging to something greater than this temporary life. Therefore, the search/desire for beauty at the time of death obligates both the church and the dying to first "*seek* this gift, and to *desire it earnestly;* and, second, to *practice* this gift as part of one's everyday spiritual discipline."[10] God's beauty will not lay dormant but is sure to spread when lifted up in joy, for "God's beauty within the world is infectious."[11]

There is a sense of mystery, something very spiritual, that occurs when providing care and accompanying the patient at the time of death. A spirituality that evokes something holy can only be described as a place of beauty. Such beauty can only be recognized as God's and beckons to the church to accompany the dying to the very gates of the other side. A demise of beauty at the time of death is a loss of awareness for God and the potential for sharing his beauty. However, it can be recovered when the church arrives and reflects the ongoing creative work of God, providing a space for his beauty.

9. Moore, *Hope of Beauty*, 169.

10. Moore, *Hope of Beauty*, 172.

11. Lane, *Ravished by Beauty*, 175.

The Early Church Application of the Second Commandment
at the Time of Death

The message of Jesus' ministry was realized in the early church by living the joint-love commandment taught by Jesus. When one loved both God and neighbor as oneself, the beauty of his message was lived out among the early church. The Mediterranean meal tradition, present in the first three centuries of the church, was the birthplace and the building blocks of community found in the house churches. The meal "offered a sense of belonging, relief from the routine and responsibilities of family life, and the company of friends."[12] Most meal associations produced more than momentary social bonding, but rather a lasting social obligation with those they met around a "table."[13] At these meals, community was built, the house church was formed, and the joint-love commandment had a place to be taught, lived, and reproduced in the life of the church.

Long-term community responsibility was the primal element of the traditional meal associations, and more specifically, house churches demonstrated God's beauty with the support at the time of death common to the meal associations. The ongoing community, built during the meal, developed relationships that naturally extended to death, the burial, and survivor assistance. The early church's adoption of the framework of the Greco-Roman Mediterranean meal associations must have seemed both a natural and acceptable place to provide the kind of community and care emulated and taught by Jesus. These early Christians "called together prostitutes, lepers, the disabled and unclean from the margins of human expendability to share at table a heavenly banquet prepared for them now."[14] This Jesus, of whom they were followers, had identified himself with the less privileged, thus establishing for all times that any discrimination of any kind is totally unacceptable, "for it is tantamount to excluding Jesus himself."[15]

Within these early Christian meal associations, both the powerfully wealthy and often the destitute poor could come together for a meal, while not as equals, but at least on the common ground of Christ's beauty, "to share a meal, spend an evening in each other's company, or comfort

---

12. Wilken, *Christians*, 36, 40.
13. Taussig, *In the Beginning*, 30.
14. Patterson, *Why the Historical Jesus*, para 9.
15. Dube, *Theological Challenges*, 537.

a grieving friend when his wife died."[16] While simply joining together for an association meal could not shift the social status of marginalized people, it did provide an opportunity for the meal participants to demonstrate their love for one another. I am somebody, I belong to something that is larger than myself, and when my time is over, I will have someone to sit with me while I die and care for my body in a dignified manner. In this kind of biblical community, dignity, value, and security, God's beauty lighted their dark world.

The Galilean peasants, among whom the first Christians found a beginning, were most interested in what the kingdom of God movement could "do for a lame child, a blind parent, a demented soul screaming its tortured isolation among the graves that mark the village fringes."[17] Among the poor, where there was no guarantee of a next meal, the kingdom of heaven found in the house church offered something that could satisfy the basic need of food and drinking water. For early Christians, the ongoing obligation until death and beyond was like many other meal associations. However, for the Christian, the association meal was more than a practical, daily reality that challenged death, prevented hunger, soothed loneliness, and removed the fear of being forgotten, but imagined death as banquet and dying as feasting in the presence of God's beauty.

The burial practices common among the poor in the first century involved a common lime pit and would have been the likely fate of Jesus' crucified body if it had not been for Joseph of Arimathaea (Matt 27:57–59). Those without the means of burial would find themselves buried in a similar "lime pit" with the multitude of other deceased peasants. The inevitable "lime pit" burial would make the burial alternative of the house church and/or meal association beautiful in its own right. When considered within the context of Christ's teaching, "Inasmuch as ye have done it unto one of the least of these . . . ye have done it unto me" (Matt 25:40), it would be easy to see God's beauty in the ongoing work of the church. Because of the work of the meal associations, "one could be confident, at the time of death, one's fellows would see to it that one received a decent burial."[18]

The community created, while eating, drinking, and planning proper burials for others, extended beyond the personal burial commitment into the everyday lives of the meal association participants. The apostles' reaction

16. Wilken, *Christians*, 36.

17. Crossan, *Life*, 1194.

18. Wilken, *Christians*, 40.

to the complaints of the widows demonstrated this ongoing care for the needs presented in the house church (Acts 6:1–4). The teachings of Jesus associated with loving and caring seem to demonstrate such holistic care:

> For I was hungry, and ye gave me meat: I was thirsty, and ye gave me drink: I was a stranger, and ye took me in: Naked, and ye clothed me: I was sick, and ye visited me: I was in prison, and ye came unto me. Then shall the righteous answer him, saying, Lord, when saw we thee hungry, and fed thee? or thirsty, and gave thee drink? When saw we thee a stranger, and took thee in? or naked, and clothed thee? Or when saw we thee sick, or in prison, and came unto thee? And the King shall answer and say unto them, Verily I say unto you, Inasmuch as ye have done it unto one of the least of these my brethren, ye have done it unto me (Matt 25:35–40).

It is worth noting in the above passage that no one is blessed or cursed for religious reasons, but rather the rebuke is to them who neglect the least, which should be welcomed as part of the house church community. Jesus clearly summarized his teaching when he said, "Thou shalt love the Lord thy God with all thy heart, and with all thy soul, and with all thy strength, and with all thy mind; and thy neighbour as thyself" (Luke 10:27). It is in this maelstrom of pain and grief among the least, the distasteful, and the horrific, that such God-inspired love shines forth as beauty. As pointed out earlier, God is beauty, his creation from the beginning is beauty, and the ongoing work of his creation (loving others) is beauty.

It was within these meal traditions the church, and/or the people of the church, built a lasting obligation, created in community and fellowship, while sharing a cup of coffee or a glass of tea and bread around a table, at a bedside, or sitting out under the trees. It is in such common places that the uncommon presence of Jesus is found, and beauty is discovered. It is in this area this writer finds the church's greatest needs; when death is possible but not imminent, the church can build community and complete unfinished earthly business by sharing stories, listening to the patients' successes and failures, laughing and crying, partaking of a meal, and sometimes just holding their hands. Many times, the dying have no one, no family, no friends, and no church. During these times, the church becomes their only community, their only family, and their eternal hope. Care at the time of death is messy, time consuming, and distressful, but Jesus desired, "That ye love one another, as I have loved you. Greater love hath no man than this, that a man lay down his life for his friends" (John 15:12–13).

In summary of this section, the first Christians were commanded to love their neighbors in the way they wished to be loved. Jesus and the early Christians lived out the principle to love their neighbors, and the first writings of the church reflected the same. While it may be difficult or impossible to find specific ancient records that demonstrate care at the death event, the community built within the house churches, the dignity attained by the participants, the ancient theology of neighbor love, the early Christian writings, the interpretation by scholars of those days, the commitment to comfort the bereaved, and the promise of a decent burial all indicate that the early church provided care to the dying and their survivors. For these Christians, caring for the sick and dying would have been an act of simple justice, an act of loving their neighbor, and a time of finding God's beauty alive and active; simply the way life and death ought to be. Beauty for the dying Christian in the first century was likely found in the neighborly love of God's creation and its ongoing work in the house church.

The Practical Application of the Second Commandment at the Time of Death

Research by this author discovered five commonalities of quality care at the time of death that were highlighted by professional caregivers: community, assessment, presence, affirmation, and listening (*See Pastoral Care Model below*).[19] These commonalities brought to the bedside of the dying a space in which to appreciate the beauty of God, his creation, and their collaborative work. Such care at the time of death is not new to the present era but can be traced back to the care provided by early Christian believers. Unfortunately, because of fifteen hundred years of an increasing effort to avoid death, community supported spiritual care at the time of death became less and less common.[20] Around the beginning of the twentieth century, this evolution came full circle when the Christian church once again reclaimed the deathbed as a place of ministry.

19. Peyton, *Finding*, 117.
20. DeSpelder and Strickland, *Last Dance*, 71.

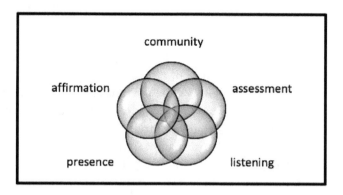

Pastoral Care Model for Use at the Time of Death

Community

The first Christians' house churches modeled biblical community by providing care when they prepared for death, gave succor during difficult times, and found beauty in suffering. Just as professional caregivers today find community essential for care at the time of death, the association meals (house churches) became the main hope for community in the dark times of the Roman Empire. "There is absolutely no question that 'community' is the one central value and the decisive category for understanding [association] meals."[21] The time spent eating the meal produced opportunity for community, equality, enduring relationships, lasting friendships, and grace/generosity/beauty among the meal's participants. Such unrestricted benefits could only be found in the kingdom of God that had come down to earth. "Thou shalt love the Lord thy God with all thy heart, and with all thy soul, and with all thy mind. This is the first and great commandment. And the second is like unto it, Thou shalt love thy neighbour as thyself. On these two commandments hang all the law and the prophets" (Matt 22:37–40).

Assessment

The wide use of the meal tradition, the many different types of associations, and the freedom to join (granted by the Roman government), demonstrate

21. Taussig, *In the Beginning*, 27.

that such choices allowed a small element of self-determination in a world where little choice was available. To have a say in their lives, and ultimately a say in who would be there when they died, both the peasant and the wealthy could choose the meal association that best provided the care they desired. While any possible record of assessment being done by care providers has been lost, such a choice before the time of death pre-determined the care that the individual would receive and served as a self-assessment, before the fact, of how they would like to die. Care at the time of death today is based upon assessments that allow for the dying to determine their exit from this world. What would you like to talk about? What would you like me to pray for? Do you have any unfinished business before you go (repentance, forgiveness, salvation assurances, debts, etc.)? What do you need to do to prepare you for the other side?

Presence

It was while attending the house church that community was found in the presence of their fellow members. Every possible kind of member was accepted, given fellowship, and awarded dignity when they sat in the presence of others. "There is neither Jew nor Greek, there is neither bond nor free, there is neither male nor female: for ye are all one in Christ Jesus" (Gal 3:28). No longer did their lack of things or positions isolate them; the presence of others at the table meant they were part of something bigger than themselves. All week long the lonely peasant was enslaved by society, spat upon by their betters, and barely made do with the little they had. The power of neighborly love drew them back to the house church every week, where they belonged to something important. The presence of the association affirmed that they had value, and for a few hours they could "share a meal, spend an evening in each other's company, or comfort a grieving friend when his wife died."[22] The church today, that equally draws people back each week into the presence of God and church family, sets the stage for similar care at the time of death. The number one fear in multiple studies at the time of death is the fear of dying alone. The church is uniquely equipped to satisfy this longing and remove this prevalent fear by simply being present. If the attending minister/caregiver of the church does not know what to do, remember this: good ministry at the time of death starts with just being present. Often no words are necessary!

22. Wilken, *Christians*, 36.

Affirmation

Setting at the common table with others in the presence of God, the early church participant was affirmed by the community (house church) of their choice: "I am not alone; I am valuable; I am welcomed; my contributions are desired." Such widespread and unrestricted affirmation was unheard of in the first century, even among the Jews. James' admonition to the house churches said it best:

> My brethren, have not the faith of our Lord Jesus Christ, the Lord of glory, with respect of persons. For if there come unto your assembly a man with a gold ring, in goodly apparel, and there come in also a poor man in vile raiment; And ye have respect to him that weareth the gay clothing, and say unto him, Sit thou here in a good place; and say to the poor, Stand thou there, or sit here under my footstool: Are ye not then partial in yourselves, and are become judges of evil thoughts? Hearken, my beloved brethren, Hath not God chosen the poor of this world rich in faith, and heirs of the kingdom which he hath promised to them that love him? But ye have despised the poor. Do not rich men oppress you, and draw you before the judgment seats? Do not they blaspheme that worthy name by the which ye are called? If ye fulfil the royal law according to the scripture, Thou shalt love thy neighbour as thyself, ye do well: But if ye have respect to persons, ye commit sin, and are convinced of the law as transgressors. For whosoever shall keep the whole law, and yet offend in one point, he is guilty of all (Jas 2:1–10).

The welcoming committee at the doors of today's churches sets the stage for affirming the value of the individual. The church cannot value/affirm a visitor's sins, lifestyles, or problems; however, the church must reflect the same value that motivated Jesus' death on the cross. He looked beyond the brokenness of humanity, saw each one created in the image of God, and laid down his life for all of humanity. When one approaches death, like no other time, she/he needs the affirmation that God found them worthy of the cross.

Listening

The house church became the channel for storytelling through which one's life stories could flow. In essence, the caregiver must extend the God who hears me! (Gen 21:14–17). "The discovery that Jesus becomes our guest when we offer hospitality [*listening*] to "the least of these" is an expression of this reciprocity . . . In the experience of reciprocity, hospitality extended [*listening*] by us to those in need becomes hospitality [*listening*] returned to us from Jesus."[23] The promise to care enough to listen today affirms care at the time of death and for the loved ones left behind, thereby magnifying the last two words of the joint-love commandment, "love thy neighbour as thyself" (Matt 22:39). Listen in a way you would desire others to listen to you!

Lessons Learned Applying the Second Commandment at the Time of Death

Our understanding of the kinds of care given at the time of death by the early church is reproduced by professional hospice workers (community, assessment, presence, affirmation, and listening). An amazing point gleaned from those interviewed was the ease in which even the layperson could join in and utilize this simple model. What does the patient want? Who is the patient's community, and how can I become a part of it? Does the patient and his/her community want me to become part of it? What can I do to affirm the patient and add value in these final moments of life? What is the patient trying to say? How hard are we listening in the patient's final moments? Even if he/she can no longer talk, the question to the family is: If the patient could talk, what would she/he most likely say to those present? These principles assist the community to see the reflection of beauty, that is already part of the patient's life, and create a sense of fullness/completeness at the end of life.

While every case is different, finding a common context is possible when the church meets the patient "where they are at" and provide community, assessment, presence, affirmation, and listening within the context in which they live and have faith. It is most often possible when one desires to reflect God's image in the face of the dying, create a space to see the holy moments of beauty that already exist, and bend with humanity as it stretches towards God's beauty. It is in that holy space where those that are able will find the God who is beautiful, who has made his creation beautiful, and whose ongoing creative work continues to shine in beauty.

The church's presence (be they single or a group) extends hope and comfort when they come alongside the dying. "From the perspective

23. Justes, *Hearing Beyond*, 94.

of the . . . cross, a ministry of presence begins to take on significantly broader meaning . . . presence now becomes theologically active."[24] It is more than just being there; rather, it is being there as a bearer of God's Spirit. Just as Jesus, in whom the Spirit dwelt (Col 2:9), culminated his life with his presence suffering with the dying on all three crosses, the church joins in this incarnation. Presence and listening gives voice to the dying: a voice to tell an interested visitor their life narrative, a voice to express their last wishes/desires, and a voice to express love to family, friends, and God. Listening, assessment, and affirmation provide a vehicle to carry the voice of the dying to its intended audience. When one is willing to listen, they enter a holy space with the dying where they can name the pain, the fear, the story, and/or whatever one wishes to name; for the voiceless this is empowering and strengthening.

Forever, oh God, you are beauty, your creation created in your image is beauty, and the beauty of your essence continues in the work of your creation! As I researched and reflected on the interaction between God and death, I was attracted to this idea of beauty. As one who has often spent time at the bedside of the dying,[25] it is my duty "to give beauty away so that the rest of the world may, in the midst of squalor, ugliness, and pain, remember that beauty is possible."[26] In my search for God's beauty, I join in the dance between patient, the family, the church, and the God of eternity.

For those inexperienced at the bedside of the dying, a "persistent longing for beauty can serve as a starting point"[27] and a place to begin the dance that will enter that space where the eternal veil is thin, and the beauty of the Lord can shine through. As the psalmist sang, there is only one thing that I will seek after . . . "to behold the beauty of the Lord" (Ps 27:4). For those experienced at the bedside of the dying, beauty is not a foreign idea, and their stories express the possibility of something strange and beautiful happening at the end of life. Understanding and appreciating that God's beauty exists, that this beauty already exists in the life of the patient, ensures that the church's visit becomes a part of the ongoing work of God's beauty. Understanding God's beauty as eternal and unchangeable brings clarity to

24. Thornton, *Broken Yet Beloved*, 17.

25. This is a conservative list of deaths in which this author was present: Hospice deaths (five hundred plus); pastoring (fifty plus); paramedic (fifty plus); assorted medical positions (one hundred plus); military (twenty-five plus).

26. O'Donohue, *Beauty*, 215.

27. O'Donohue, *Beauty*, 158.

ministry at the time of death, when one holds up a mirror in which to reflect God's image, creating space to see the *imago dei* reflected in the patient. This reflection invites the dying to join, bending towards God's beauty, as plants that bend together towards the sunlight.

Understanding one's beauty in the light of God's beauty, and the work of life as the co-creation of both God and humankind, generates a sense God's ongoing incarnational work. Those attending death, as the *imago dei*, holding up a mirror to the dying, who are also the *imago dei*, can reflect their joint beauty as people created by the God who is beauty. The patients' ability to see their reflection in the beauty of the church's presence can be the opening through which to see God's beauty at the time of death. "As admittedly finite creatures, we can incarnate God's love in a powerful way to those in crisis . . . so the presence of the [church] becomes a window through which the infinite Source of hope can be glimpsed."[28]

Being created in God's image brings renewed meaning to the life of any individual, but is especially important to the dying, who often spend time questioning the value of their life. Helping the dying remember that in the beginning they were beautifully created in God's image, and that God's desire for their life has always been the ongoing demonstration of God's beauty, becomes the important work at the time of death. Despite the life lived, God's beauty had not lain dormant; but when a life is reflected by a church that lifts it up in joy, one can see the multitude of attempts that God has made to shine forth his beauty. For the patient and/or family to have these moments of beauty, they need a church who loves them enough to take the time to pursue beauty in difficult places. Individuals who are willing to stand/sit by the dying, listen to their stories, and affirm the patient's life as valuable and beautiful, can declare: "In that moment of your life, the beauty of God broke forth!" Sometimes the beauty is in that moment, when the patient and family are giving voice to the life of the dying, a space in which they can together see the beauty of God, despite the pain and suffering by the cause of death.

Finally, it is important that we truly value the dying person as the *imago dei*. Not because it is one's job, not because somebody must do it, and not because it is what the church does, but because even the least of our neighbors are already the creation of God; therefore, we are commanded to love them as ourselves. Since all are created in the image of God, the beauty exists and must be lifted in a demonstration of love for

28. Ciampa, *God-Talk*, 33.

God and a love for neighbor. Such love is the ultimate sense of God's beauty at work in the world. The presence of the church must say to the dying, as the valued creation of God and loved by the church: this is not the end, this is not the last word on their life, and that all have this eternal hope in Christ (1 Cor 15:19).

A few years ago, in a single day, I was called to a series of particularly difficult deathbed scenes. All three, in their own way, were the most horrible deaths I had ever imagined. It was a day of dealing with one patient's uncontrolled pain, another's incredible family dysfunction, and a family's grief over the rape/murder of a child. On a day like this, when even the experienced considers a different form of ministry, it is the memory of God's beauty that draws one back to the bedside of another dying patient. Thankfully, there are other memories that remain of others who saw beauty in their reflection as God's image. There are those recollections of times, when space was created, we enjoyed holy moments examining the beauty of God that existed in their story. I have felt the warmth of sunlight as together we bent as a plant toward the beauty of God's ongoing work. It is in this incarnational ministry the church, who wishes to be Jesus for the dying, can walk as emissaries of God and speak peace and hope into the lives of the grieving families. "Pastoral care is, in essence, surprisingly simple. It has one fundamental aim: to help people know love, both as something to be received and as something to give."[29] It is in the knowing and giving of love that beauty so naturally exists.

Pastor Levi drove across town to the nursing home where Fred's family had gathered at the death bed of their loved one. As Pastor Levi drove, he thought about what he knew about Fred. When Betty first came to church she would bring her father, Fred, with her on special occasions (e.g., Christmas, Easter, etc.). Fred was so old and frail that he didn't come very often and, at first, made no move to pray or worship. About a year ago, after an Easter drama at the church, an altar call was given and, much to everyone's surprise, down the aisle came Fred with tears running down his face. Betty and others joined around him and, before long, Fred was filled with the Spirit of God while the church rejoiced. In a few moments, Betty led her father off to be baptized, and that was the best Easter program the church ever had. The next week, Fred's health took a turn for the worse and,

29. Campbell, *Professionalism*, 11.

before long, hospice had been called in to assist with the difficult last few months. Sadly, Fred had never been back to church!

As Pastor Levi pulled up at the nursing home, he tried to remember the kinds of pastoral things that the hospice blog recommended at the time of death (community, assessment, presence, affirmation, and listening). It sounded easy enough, but what will everyone think of my efforts? Only Betty came to his church, and he knew nothing of the rest of the family. After stopping at the nurses' station to let the nurse that called know that he had arrived, Pastor Levi walked down to the hospice room. The silence of the room was deafening, and the family was sitting in chairs around the outer walls. Betty came immediately, weeping, to greet her pastor. Together they went to empty chairs on both sides of the bed. Much to Pastor Levi's surprise, Fred's eyes were open, and he recognized the pastor of Betty's church.

As Pastor Levi sat down, Fred's wrinkled hand reached for his as he said, "I'm so sorry! I never got to become a member of the church. I really planned to after that last Sunday . . ."

Pastor Levi had a moment of panic as he tried to remember what he was supposed to do . . . and which one of the five steps was the most important? Were they steps or just principles? Well, he finally decided that he would take them as they came, and listening seemed to be the first thing to do. Pastor Levi leaned over Fred, so he didn't have to speak loudly, and said, "Fred, tell me about what happened to you on that Sunday?"

Fred grinned despite the pain, "Wow . . . why did I wait so long? I don't really know what happened, but the Easter drama made me realize that Jesus died for me! I was so confused. How could he do it for me? I have always been a little wild, an unfaithful husband, and an absent father. Why would Jesus die for me? Next thing I knew, I was walking down the aisle! When I realized I was at the front, I started to go back and realized a bunch of people were blocking my way. Someone said to tell God I was sorry and, while I was trying to, I began to speak in a language I had never heard before. Betty said it was the Holy Spirit and that I should be baptized . . . well, you know the rest. After I was baptized, Betty took me home and I got real sick . . . I never got to go back. I'm so sorry! I should have started a long time ago. I might have had a life worth giving to God!"

By this time Betty and Pastor Levi had tears running down their faces. The only thing Pastor Levi could think of was how beautiful this story was. "Fred, that story is so beautiful! It

*doesn't matter the life you lived. God found you worth saving!"
As Pastor Levi realized the family had gathered close as Fred told
his story, he said, "Fred, why don't we just lift up our voices and
thank God for this amazing story!" Pastor realized that this must
be God's purpose!*

*Betty and Pastor Levi lifted Fred's hands and together they be-
gan to thank God for this moment of beauty. Pastor Levi knew the
family didn't have many good memories, but now the last memories
could beckon to them across time to something hopeful for them
all. As they prayed, and tears of the family flowed freely, they all
watched as Fred's smile grew larger and larger, and finally, they
knew that he was gone. After a period of time, during which Pastor
Levi hugged and prayed individually for many that were there, they
each began to leave, starting the difficult process of grieving.*

*When most had left and only Betty and her brother were left,
Pastor Levi said goodbye.*

*As he turned to leave, Betty's brother said, "Thank you, Pastor,
I'll see you on Sunday! I must know what my father was talking
about!"*

10

The Second Commandment in Immigrant Care

Forasmuch then as God gave them the like gift as he did unto us, who believed on the Lord Jesus Christ; what was I, that I could withstand God? When they heard these things, they held their peace, and glorified God, saying, Then hath God also to the Gentiles granted repentance unto life.

—ACTS 11:17–18

Pastor Levi sat at his desk with his head in his hands, thinking about all the pressing things he had to do: he had to prepare a funeral for Fred, he still hadn't done anything (other than pray) about Jim and Sharon, his wife had hardly seen him in recent days, and he had given no thought to services on Sunday. While he sat there, he heard timid footsteps coming through the auditorium towards his office, and a fifteen-year-old girl (who he presumed was part of the Guatemalans that were in church last Sunday) stuck her head through the open door.

"Excuse me, mister," she said nervously, "Are you busy?"

Pastor Levi chuckled to himself and thought, "There must be a better word for my situation than busy?" However, he spoke to the girl, "What can I help you with?"

"Well, sir," as she slowly looked around his office in awe, "My father would like to talk with you."

Pastor Levi, now standing, looked quickly out the door of his office towards the empty auditorium. "Where is he?"

As she turned to hurry out of the auditorium, she called back over her shoulder, "He is in the car! I will get him." In a few minutes she returned with a middle-aged, dark-skinned man.

As he approached Pastor Levi, he held out his hand and spoke in a language the pastor had never heard. Pastor Levi was confused; he knew enough Spanish to know this was not the language he had studied. As he momentarily puzzled about what to say/do, the girl spoke up and said, "He said, 'My name is Babajide. I am pleased to meet you!' He does not speak English, mister, but I will translate for you."

Pastor Levi was shocked, but responded, "It is good to meet you both. My name is Joe Levi. I am the pastor of this church. I'm sorry, but I didn't recognize your Spanish."

"So very sorry, Pastor," she quickly said after translating it to her father, "We are not Spanish Guatemalans. We are Mayan Guatemalans, and we speak the native Yucatec Maya language. Is this okay?"

"Yes, of course. Come in." They entered the office and sat on the couch. Pastor Levi remembered what he had learned when studying pastoral care, and he knew, if he was going to provide good care for these newcomers, it must start with an interpretation of the care needed. Again, listening seemed to be what was needed at this time. "Tell me about yourselves and what I can do for you."

During the next hour, Pastor Levi realized he had a lot to learn about the culturally and linguistically differences of the Guatemalan immigrants that were moving into his town, and now sat in his office. Like many other refugees trying to gain access to the United States, indigenous Guatemalan immigrants have been characterized as "crossfire refugees," caught between two warring factions in a civil war in their home country, belonging to neither.

The non-indigenous Guatemalan government, that resulted from the 1996 peace accords, continues to oppress the largely indigenous rural population in much the same way as their predecessors. At times, the new government attempted to ethnically cleanse the country by massacring entire indigenous villages, eliminating church workers in indigenous areas, and systematically "kidnapping, torturing, and killing hundreds of indigenous leaders."[1] Consequently, such an unbearable life in rural, indig-

---

1. Wellmeier, *Santa Eulalia's People*, 102–3.

enous Guatemala produced the currently high rate of indigenous immigration to the United States.[2]

For over an hour Babajide (strong one), with his daughter, Abha (bright one), translating, told the story of their year-long journey north and another year spent in a camp in Mexico, waiting for the United States to let them enter. Pastor Levi learned they had been part of a Christian group in the hill country of Guatemala and were looking for a place to go to church: a place that would allow them to both be part of the English service and to also hold services in their native language and honor their native traditions.

That night Pastor Levi woke up from a familiar dream. It was a dream he experienced often over the last forty years; a dream that he had less and less over the years. A dream where he was a missionary to a group of brown-skinned people. Many years before, he had tried to raise money and learn Spanish, but time, a growing family, and responsibilities had dissolved any hope he had. But now, the mission field had come to his town . . .

ACCORDING TO THE UNITED Nations, 232 million people worldwide qualify as diaspora/immigrant peoples (diaspora peoples being defined as forcefully displaced peoples due to economics, politics, health, religion, war, etc.). The United States is the largest recipient of such displaced peoples with 50.6 million as of 2014 (15.3 percent of the United States' population of 329 million; this statistic increased by 17 million since the year 2000).[3] Among recent immigrating people worldwide, the Christian religion makes up the majority faith of those displaced (49 percent, or 113.68 million), but of those immigrating to the United States, a far greater percentage are Christians (74 percent, or 32 million).[4] This tragic, forced, modern migration of large population groups gives Christians in the United States a golden opportunity to fulfill the Great Commission of Christ, "Go ye therefore, and teach all nations, baptizing them" (Matt 28:19–20). "For Christians who participate in God's redemptive purposes, the migration of people, whether forced or voluntary, should be viewed not as accidental, but part of God's sovereign plan."[5]

2. Bennett, *I Became More Maya*, 2.

3. Migration Data Portal, *2020 Data*.

4. Pew Research Institute, *Faith on the Move*.

5. Im and Yong, *Global Diasporas*, 148.

The command to baptize and make disciples of all nations has found a great opportunity among the unreached in America's own backyard. Many churches also assist with the vast logistical needs of their daily lives (housing, food, education, safety, etc.). Unfortunately, the overwhelming spiritual and logistical needs have largely precluded the ability to provide the broad-spectrum care needed by them and mandated by the biblical command to love one's neighbor as oneself. Therefore, a biblical argument that better emulates the care provided by Jesus and the early church must be built on a foundation of the second commandment. This chapter will build upon the previous chapters of this book and explain the church's biblical mandate for involvement with (and care for) immigrant populations.

Considering a Definition for Immigrant Care

It is imperative, if one is to fully understand the biblical mandate for immigrant care based upon the first and second commandments (love God, love neighbor), one must first know what is meant by the utilization of the term care (as in pastoral care and immigrant care). Carol Wise, an early pastoral care theologian, defined pastoral care simply, "Effective pastoral care, that is, meeting a person at the point of his need, demands the pastor become involved in the very existence and predicament of the person, his tensions, suffering, meanings, values, joys."[6] Other early pastoral care researchers claimed the pastoral caregiver is the orchestrator, the holder of "the personal dialogue between creator and creature"[7] and the facilitator of the abiding role of the Spirit when providing pastoral care. A further development saw pastoral care as more than an intermediary between God and man, but also as the organizer of care in the Christian community. "Pastoral care [is] in the center of the dialogical space between the communal story of the Christian community and the many life stories of people who are in some way related to the Christian community."[8]

A final element important to loving and caring for immigrant populations is the use of *holistic* to envision care that must intentionally include a full human range of care for the volitional, emotional, social, physical, mental, and spiritual needs.[9] The lack of holistic care among immigrants is often

6. Wise, *Meaning*, 14.
7. Gerkin, *Introduction*, 69.
8. Gerkin, *Introduction*, 111–12.
9. Culbertson, *Caring*, 5.

due to the overwhelming basic physical needs (housing, food, safety, etc.) and the often-vast spiritual needs (sometimes including a lack of knowledge and faith in Christ). Other real, felt needs, that are less apparent, are sometimes overlooked, or even ignored, and can cause long-term health and mental issues. Therefore, a concise understanding of holistic care in this chapter includes the church caring for a wide range of needs for the immigrants in their neighborhood (at the point of their needs) with the hope of integrating their story into the Christian story and tradition. Only when we love the new neighbor from abroad as we love our selves, will they feel welcomed and become fully part of the local Christian community.

A Biblical Argument for Loving/Caring for One's Immigrant Neighbors

"The Spirit of the Lord is upon me, because he hath anointed me to preach the gospel to the poor; he hath sent me to heal the brokenhearted, to preach deliverance to the captives, and recovering of sight to the blind, to set at liberty them that are bruised, To preach the acceptable year of the Lord" (Luke 4:18–19; Isa 61:1–3). This prophesied and expressed mission of Jesus, the son of God, was foretold by the Old Testament prophet Isaiah and deliberately claimed in the New Testament. This mission of God provides a place to begin our consideration of the church's responsibility to provide care in the modern era. The preaching of the Gospel to the poor guarantees access to the son of God by all people (including the immigrants). Healing, deliverance, recovery, and liberty demonstrated that Christ came to do more than just share salvation, but his love included a wider range of care for emotional, social, physical, mental, and spiritual needs.

Isaiah presented this mission to the Israelites at the end of the Babylonian captivity to emphasize the range of responsibility to the Israelites returning to Palestine. They must not return in their post-captivity with the same pre-captivity lack of concern for the poor, the brokenhearted, the captives, the blind, the bruised, and the mourners. Jesus claimed Isaiah's mission of God for the Israelites (a mission they never fulfilled) and lived it out as the focal point of his earthly ministry by declaring that the *not yet* had become *now*; "This day is this scripture fulfilled in your ears" (Luke 4:21). Jesus was calling the New Testament church to follow him in fulfilling this holistic care, based upon the joint-love commandment, for all of humanity.

The judgment God sent the Israelites at the hand of the Assyrians was because they turned aside the needy from judgment, ignored the rights of the poor, preyed upon widows, and robbed orphans (Isa 10:1–6). This behavior was in stark contrast to the post-captivity passage above. Repeatedly, prophet after prophet warned Israel of their lack of care and concern for the disadvantaged, which included the stranger/alien in their midst, and yet they went unchanged into captivity. Their return from captivity was an opportunity to begin with a holistic view of all people, and the prophet wanted to remind them of their missional obligations as God's people engaged in God's world for the sake of the whole of God's creation.[10]

The majority of the biblical story includes "migrants of one sort or another, so it is not surprising that God gives us a great deal of guidance about interacting with immigrants."[11] This mission of God to all peoples extended from the Creator's command to the initial creation to replenish the whole earth (Gen 1:28) and is culminated with Christ's acceptance of the mission, demonstrated above. This care for all humanity can further be established by understanding that the Bible is a book about immigration. Whether they were a landless/wandering people before Egypt, slaves in Egypt, a kingdom fighting for their place/land, enslaved again in Babylon, or oppressed by the Romans, and whether they were Israelite or Christian, God's people have always been a displaced/persecuted people. "If we take all the [Bible] stories together, we have examples of almost every known form of migration, voluntary and involuntary."[12] Even in the few years of peace during the days of the Kingdom of Israel/Judah, they were cautioned to remember the days in Egypt when the Lord God had redeemed them. Furthermore, this Egyptian memory was the motivation behind their care and treatment of the stranger (immigrant), the fatherless, and the widow that were in their midst (Deut 24:18–22).

While the redemption of all peoples is clearly accepted as the responsibility of the church, too often churches have implemented evangelism without considering the longer-term need for holistic care. This responsibility must include the care of immigrants who have moved into the backyard of the church. In the Old Testament, the people of Israel were responsible for providing such care to the least and, by extension, to the stranger/proselyte who had moved into their midst. The Law repeatedly states that such

10. Wright, *Mission of God*, 23.

11. Soerens and Yang, *Welcoming*, 86.

12. Im and Yong, *Global Diasporas*, 19.

care included both the least of the Israelites (the poor, the disabled, the fatherless, and the widows) and the foreigner living among them (Exod 12:19, 20:10; Lev 6:29, 17:8–9, 19:18, 33, 20:2, 24:16; Num 9:14). Similarly, the prophet Isaiah called on the eunuch (considered Israel's least) and the foreigner, both of whom had joined themselves to the returning people of God, not to feel as if they were inferior or dispensable, but to take full advantage of the care provided by God's people (Isa 56:1–6). While the care of immigrating people "is important in the Old Testament, it is fundamental to the message of the New Testament as well."[13]

In the New Testament one sees Christ's inclusion of immigrants in claiming Isaiah's mission of God in several ways. Christ's own ministry was among the very least of humanity and refers to this same Isaiah passage to demonstrate to the imprisoned John that he was indeed the one who came to fulfill Isaiah's prophecy, "how that the blind see, the lame walk, the lepers are cleansed, the deaf hear, the dead are raised, to the poor the gospel is preached" (Luke 7:22–23). As demonstrated in the above Old Testament passages, this New Testament care was also not limited to the least, but to non-Jewish immigrants as well. Jesus' ministry extended to the Samaritans (Luke 17:6; John 4), Canaanites (Mark 3:18), a Syro-Phoenician woman (Matt 15:22–28), and Romans (Luke 7:6). The healing of the Syro-Phoenician woman's daughter, who was "triply polluted—foreign, female, and demon possessed,"[14] is especially instructive in demonstrating Christ's willingness to extend care outside all restrictions of culture, national origin, religious inhibitions, or political boundaries.

The early church also lived out Christ's Great Commission (Matt 28:19) by embracing the Isaiah-mission of God to the very least and the non-Jewish people among whom they were forced to live. From the very outpouring of the Holy Spirit on the day of Pentecost upon *all* flesh, God demonstrated this principle in the inclusion on that day of men and women, young and old, rich and poor, slave and free, Jew and Gentile, with a multi-ethnic crowd from more than fourteen nations (Acts 2). One sees the disciples' dual commitment to fulfill the teachings of the resurrected Christ in their care for both the least and the stranger/foreigner when they cared for the Grecian widows (Acts 6:1–4), when they embraced the full inclusion of all the hearers of Cornelius' household (Acts 10:44), and in Paul's gentile collection for the poor of Jerusalem (Acts 24:17). Peter's words and actions were

13. Carroll, *Christians*, 79.
14. Snyder, *Asylum-Seeking*, 171.

instructive for all the church to follow, "Of a truth I perceive that God is no respecter of persons: But in every nation he that feareth him, and worketh righteousness, is accepted with him" (Acts 10:34–35).

James refused to separate the care of the spiritually poor from the physically poor (Jas 2:2–8), stating that this is especially important and, in doing so, would "miss the ministry of Jesus himself."[15] James was writing to an audience of immigrants, and therefore his refusal to ignore the social impact of their cultural and geographic upheaval is especially important to the church today, when ministering to and caring for immigrants. Finally, John's prophecy is clear that in the last days God will gather and judge the saints and sinners alike from among all nations and among all classes of people scattered throughout the world (Rev 7:9, 11:9, 13:16). It can be argued that the church of Laodicea lacked a willingness to provide the kind of care outlined in the Isaiah 61 mission that was embraced by Christ; not knowing that they themselves were wretched, miserable, poor, blind, and naked (brokenhearted, captive, blind, and bruised). The church of Laodicea was counseled to purchase the purity of Christ (to be like Jesus), that they would be rich and clothed with white raiment, and then the shame of their lacking would go away, that they might see (Rev 3:17–18).

In keeping with the theme of this book, the second commandment, which commands the love of one's neighbor, is the underpinning of all the above Scriptures in both testaments. Jesus summed it up this way, "Thou shalt love the Lord thy God with all thy heart, and with all thy soul, and with all thy mind. This is the first and great commandment. And the second is like unto it, Thou shalt love thy neighbour as thyself. On these two commandments hang all the law and the prophets" (Matt 22:37–40). And the apostle Paul echoed it, "For this, Thou shalt not commit adultery, Thou shalt not kill, Thou shalt not steal, Thou shalt not bear false witness, Thou shalt not covet; and if there be any other commandment, it is briefly comprehended in this saying, namely, Thou shalt love thy neighbour as thyself" (Rom 13:9). The exhaustive use of the joint-love commandment extends from the Old Testament Law (Lev 19:18) to the ministry of Jesus (Matt 5:44, 19:19, 22:39; Mark 12:31–33; Luke 10:27–31) and into the life of the early church (Rom 13:9–10; Gal 5:14; Jas 2:8).

The call for holistic care (meeting immigrating peoples holistically at the point of their felt needs) is based upon Christ's example of his love for the least and can be demonstrated throughout the Old and New

15. Dempster et al., *Globalization*, 17.

Testaments. The joint-love commandment is the foundation of faith for both Jew and Christian and found in the words/works of the prophets, the Christ, the disciples, the first church, and the prophesies concerning the end of time. The immigrant has captured "the very heart of God's saving work, no matter when, where, or among whom."[16] With certainty, the joint-love commandment (love for God and love for neighbor) offers principles that guide the church today in considering the current immigration dilemma and should influence the response of the church "in a way that reflects God's love, compassion and justice."[17]

Implications for Utilizing the Second Commandment Among Immigrant Populations

In the early 2000s, many immigrants from the non-Christian Somali Bantu people in Africa were forced, by years of war, to move to the United States. Four thousand African immigrants (many of them Somali Bantu) were moved to Lewiston, Maine, and this migration changed the city forever. There were mixed feelings and opinions about this migration by the people and churches of this small city of thirty-five thousand people. The opinion early on by some of those living there was negative, and people lined the streets outside the city offices in protests of so many people "from away" moving into Lewiston's backyard. Some of these negative feelings and protests included clergy members from the community. At this same time, the press was showcasing clergy who were providing humanitarian assistance and a wide range of pastoral care services. Ten years later it became clear that the Somali migration had revitalized the city and saved them from certain bankruptcy when the housing bubble burst in 2008.[18] What is also clear is that a vast number of the Somalis have become Christians, almost exclusively in the few churches that welcomed and assisted them. Those churches are now bursting at the seams with Somali Christians.

On the surface, I am uncomfortable with the pragmatic implications of the above news story that seem to emphasize the numbers in church growth and economic stability for Lewiston. However, behind the numbers is the conversion of many immigrants to Christianity who were formally Muslim, the binding up of the brokenhearted masses of their war-torn world, the

16. Im and Yong, *Global Diasporas*, 261.

17. Soerens and Yang, *Welcoming*, 86.

18. Ellison, *Lewiston, Maine*.

proclaiming of liberty to those captive for years in fear and instability, and the opening of the prisons of poverty, disease, hunger, and death. As wise stewards who recognized that the Lord had provided opportunities in just such a time, some were intentional about ministering to the Somali Bantu people and changed more than a church's growth curve or a city's economic outcome. The Somali Bantu people's eternity was impacted by care for the "new" least in the backyards of a few visionary Christians.

Once again, we must consider the definition of holistic care from earlier in the story of America's new immigrant neighbors. Holistic care is meeting these immigrant peoples at the point of their felt needs, while integrating their story into the Christian story and tradition, and while making them feel welcomed and part of the larger Christian community. While such care cannot be subdivided in application, for the sake of discussing the parts of the whole and its implication for diaspora care, it can/will be divided into three major parts: care, story, and hospitality.

Caring for Felt Needs

The first implication of the definition is in the providing of care in response to their felt needs. Determining felt needs is the result of relationships built over time with mutual respect, trust, and the neighborly love of the time-valued story of the Good Samaritan (Luke 10:25–37). It is in this kind of committed relationship that one can discover the self-determining needs of the immigrants that are moving into our backyard. Allowing immigrants to self-determine their needs "ensures greater ownership of the . . . experience."[19] Greater ownership and self-determination ensure that the newcomers to our community feel valued, welcomed, and part of the combined local culture. Such ownership, developed in a mutually submissive relationship, can create the equal sense of value found in a people created in the *imago dei* (Gen 1:26). Finally, immigrants' attention will turn to eternal needs once their pressing, immediate needs are satisfied (safety, health, food, housing, employment, etc.).

19. Wan and Tira, *Missions Practice*, 100.

Caring for Immigrant Stories

The second implication of the definition is in the integration of their migrant story and traditions into the larger migrant Christian story. As pilgrims (the church) and strangers (the immigrants) together (each with an individual story, but together in God's story), both caregiver and care receiver desire a better country. Together they must pursue that heavenly city that has been prepared for both by the God who is not ashamed to be their God (Heb 11:13–16). This unashamed God's redemptive story brings understanding and gives purpose to the broken story of humanity by including our stories in his eternal story. "For the Christian pastor or the Christian community as a whole, the primary language of care is a language of the Christian story and tradition." Caregivers find themselves with a sacred trust "between loyalty to and representation of the Christian story, on the one hand, and emphatic attention to the particularity of life stories, on the other."[20]

Caring with Hospitality

The third implication of the definition is providing hospitality, so they feel welcomed and part of the worldwide Christian community. "The church is a place to belong and become—to become more like Christ. Thus it is a place both of affirmation and accountability, of comfort and care-fronting."[21] The hearts and doors of the church must open in such a Christian way that the immigrant feels a welcome and a home-away-from-home in a world that has daily become increasingly hostile and foreign. This gives the church the opportunity to welcome the stranger, spoken of in the Scripture by Christ, when he said, "Verily I say unto you, Inasmuch as ye have done it unto one of the least of these my brethren, ye have done it unto me" (Matt 25:38–40).

Loving one's neighbor should be the "guiding principle both in personal interaction and as we think about the structural issues that affect our immigrant neighbors."[22] Each of the three major implications of our *holistic care* definition (care, story, and hospitality) must be founded upon the guiding principle of God's joint-love commandment (love God and

20. Gerkin, *Introduction*, 111–12.

21. Kellemen, *Gospel Conversations*, 57.

22. Soerens and Yang, *Welcoming*, 92.

love neighbor) (Matt 22:37–38). "As the first family of God under the New Covenant, the early Christians cared for the needs of each other . . . care was extended above all to widows, orphans, the elderly and sick, those incapable of working and the unemployed, prisoners, and exiles."[23] Jesus told his followers, "By this shall all men know that ye are my disciples, if ye have love one to another" (John 13:35). Love for one another and the supplying of one another's needs "is the key component in a formative Christian environment."[24]

Lessons Learned When Applying the Second Commandment to Immigrant Populations

Considering one last time Christ's mission in Luke 4:18, on which this argument has been established, one finds that God's mission to the nations is at the foundation of the mission of God in Isa 61:1–3. This mission to the poor, the broken, the captives, the blind, and the bruised, was embraced by Christ at the outset of his ministry and must be lived out in the ministry of his church. The gospel to the poor, healing to the brokenhearted, deliverance to the captives, sight to the blind, and liberty to the bruised provide a holistic picture of the kind of care for the immigrants and the lifelong residents of our communities. Holistic caregivers must resist the tendency or inclination to provide isolated care as though the individual could be separated into so many pieces. The hungry that darken the doors of our churches are often hungry for food, friendship, fellowship, and an infilling of God's Spirit.

The massive immigration problem that has come to America's backyard, while being larger than any other historical migration, has provided the church with an unprecedented opportunity to provide care to people groups that have previously been unreachable. This opportunity to love like Jesus and the early church makes missionaries of us all. Holistic care can never be less than a salvation/evangelistic response to the people without Christ that now live around us. However, the daily logistical needs of food, housing, health, and financial anxieties of our broken world must be the concerns of a church community that loves their neighbors. When providing care to immigrant populations, a wide range of volitional, emotional, social, physical, mental, and spiritual needs must be considered (*see chapter*

23. Boone, *Community and Worship*, 7.
24. Boone, *Community and Worship*, 7-8.

6 for more on this). While providing care, the church needs a clear understanding and an unshakable motivation from the biblical mandate to provide care to immigrants, strangers, and the least of our privileged society. "And if a stranger sojourn with thee in your land, ye shall not vex him. But the stranger that dwelleth with you shall be unto you as one born among you, and thou shalt love him as thyself; for ye were strangers in the land of Egypt: I am the LORD your God" (Lev 19:33–37).

Pastor Levi knew that his church would never be the same if he welcomed the Guatemalans into First Church. He knew what some of the people in the church would say. He might even lose some of the people that had been there for a very long time. But Pastor Levi knew that God was calling First Church to be bigger, better, different, more biblical, more . . . Yes, that's the key! More like Jesus! If Jesus had a church, one thing is certain, the Pharisees, the wealthy, and the politically connected would not have attended. Pastor Levi had to chuckle; he had been trying to build a church where the "good people" of his town would be comfortable. The result was still the same, few of the "good people" ever came. Unfortunately, since church was designed for good, normal, and well-adjusted people, there was no welcome mat for the poor, the broken, the captives, the blind, and the bruised. Maybe if he built a church for the poor, the broken, the captives, the blind, and the bruised . . . maybe there was no such thing as good people and the world was completely full of poor, broken, blind, and bruised captives! Pastor Levi could feel the Son rising over the church's horizon.

11

Conclusions—Go and do thou likewise!

Take care of him; and whatsoever thou spendest more, when I come again, I will repay thee. Which now of these three, thinkest thou, was neighbour unto him that fell among the thieves? And he said, He that shewed mercy on him. Then said Jesus unto him, Go, and do thou likewise.

—LUKE 10:35–37

GO AND DO THOU likewise! Two parts . . . two principles . . . First, go! Isolation is not the answer, nor is it the desire of Christ for the world today. Second, do it the same way! Copy the Good Samaritan! Go and do! Go and love! Go and care! Go and sacrifice! The church today must go and, while they are going, they must love (even the least desirable). In these conclusions, I acknowledge that they may be repetitious and for some they may be challenging! If you have read the book, you will only find more of the same in this final summary chapter. But if you are like many and have jumped to the conclusions to see if it agrees with your theology or if it is worth reading, I am reaching for you in hopes that what you see here will make you go back and read more of the book. Join me in a world of hate, isolation, and individualism. Join me in going as I love God and living God's love unto others.

Summary of Section One—Chapters 2–5

For Christians, the Bible is the first and final authority for doctrine, theology, missional pursuits, life principles, and historic examples for those that desire to follow Christ. In section one we have considered the exhaustive biblical record that establishes the joint-love commandment (love God and love neighbor) as the foundation for the entire biblical text (*chapter 2*). The church is called (missionally) to follow (emulate) the life and example of Christ (*chapter 3*). The early church's behavior, from the very beginning, demonstrates their understanding of Jesus as the Christ, son of the living God (*chapter 4*). Finally, the hot spots of modern Pentecostal revival around the world demonstrated that the church that loves God and loves their neighbor—in obedience to the doctrine, theology, and mission—results in growth, strength, and revival.

Biblical Foundations

Americans are part of a Christian world that has become very comfortable with the first commandment (at least as far as they understand it) that commands us to love God with all of our heart, all of our soul, and all of our mind (Matt 22:37). Yet the body of Christ must examine the world around them that is often void of the second commandment of Christ, "Love your neighbor as yourself" (Matt 22:39), and the effect this has had upon the church. This problem is not isolated to those in the world; within the ranks of Christianity are church members that are lonely and without an active community to support them. The need for obedience to the second commandment is urgently felt in our day and will be greatly needed in the turbulent times before the rapture. What is needed in the Christian world today is Christians that incorporate a love for God and a love for others into their church, their lives, and their community.

One cannot fully comprehend the role of the second commandment unless he understands the relationship between the first and the second commandments. The command to "love the Lord thy God with all thy heart, and with all thy soul, and with all thy mind" is how God equips the church to love their neighbors (Matt 22:37–40). When the church fully loves God— who lived a life loving his neighbors—it becomes equally easy to love one's neighbor in the same manner. Quite simply, the way to love God is to love the world he died to save (John 3:16). Jesus said it this way, "Come, ye blessed of my Father, inherit the kingdom prepared for you from the foundation of the world: For I was an hungered, and ye gave me meat: I was thirsty, and ye gave me drink: I was a stranger, and ye took me in: Naked, and ye clothed me: I was sick, and ye visited me: I was in prison, and ye came unto me" (Matt 25:34–36). The righteous were astonished and replied with the question: When did we do any of these things? Jesus' reply mirrors the second commandment when he tells the righteous, "Inasmuch as ye have done *it* unto one of the least of these my brethren, ye have done *it* unto me" (Matt 25:37–40). If one desires to love God with all his heart, soul, and mind, the way to do this is by reading the command to love God in context with the command to love one's neighbor. Jesus knew how subjective (variable interpretations) loving God was for people limited by their humanity and provided a second commandment that is like loving God (Matt 22:39).

The love for one's neighbors is not left up to the individual's discretion, but rather was specific with two very important principles. The first principle was to love (not like) one's neighbor; the second principle was to love one's neighbor in the same way one loves himself. For only when one has loved his neighbor (who could be the least of these) as himself has he loved the Lord with all his heart, soul, and mind. Conversely, it is true, "Inasmuch as ye did *it* not to one of the least of these, ye did *it* not to me" (Matt 25:40). The punishment for not fulfilling the second commandment and the reward for loving one's neighbor is plain, "these shall go away into everlasting punishment: but the righteous into life eternal" (Matt 25:46).

It is equally important that one understands that loving one's neighbor is not possible unless one truly does love the Lord with all his heart, soul, and mind. Empty and hollow neighborliness only creates hard feelings and a sense of obligation/indebtedness among neighbors. However, when the church is motivated to love her neighbors because of her consuming love for the Savior, community and fellowship are created. Neighbor-love is driven by the combination of the first and the second commandments. Only when Christians are consumed with loving God can they fulfill the obligation to also love their neighbor. The Scriptures further warn that if Christians only love those who love them back, they are no different than non-Christians (Matt 5:46–47). Two thousand years later, Christ is still asking the church to gather to him, by loving their neighbor, the least, on whom he promised to pour out his Spirit (Acts 2:17). Often Christians separate these divinely joined commandments and do harm to the intent and mission of God. These two commandments must become one great commandment!

Let there be no mistake, the second commandment was not, and is not today, a suggestion. Repeatedly, throughout both the New and the Old Testaments, loving one's neighbor is referred to as a commandment. Jesus spoke to the lawyer, who stated that both the first and the second commandments were the requirement to obtain the kingdom of God, and said, "Thou hast answered right: this do, and thou shalt live" (Luke 10:28). There is an urgent call to obedience that runs throughout the New Testament for the church to love her neighbors like Christ did: "daily, persistently, practically. Jesus modeled servanthood, self-sacrifice, and special concern for the poor and neglected."[1] *To be like Jesus* must become more than a song and/or a clever saying. His command to us was, "Go, and do thou likewise" (Luke 10:37).

The Church

Jesus condenses the six hundred and thirteen different commandments in the law of Moses and all the writings of the prophets in one joined-love commandment called the first and second commandment (Matt 22:40). There are hundreds of verses in the Bible that require God's people to reach out to the poor, the widow, the stranger, the least, etc. This vast amount of biblical support for loving others reinforces what this author has established as the basis for theology: love for God and a love for others. Furthermore, the history of the church down through the ages, regardless of what name it bore, has found success in the hands of the second commandment. The church knew that the power of inclusion was developed when parishioners loved both God and others. Loving one's neighbor develops committed, responsible, and dedicated saints/ministers, as well as those that benefit from such ministry.

Another caution from this section is, "It is a delusion to substitute love of God for love of neighbor, and a delusion to substitute love of neighbor for love of God."[2] One cannot deny the Scripture, "If a man say, I love God, and hateth his brother, he is a liar: for he that loveth not his brother whom he hath seen, how can he love God whom he hath not seen? And this commandment have we from him, That he who loveth God love his brother also" (1 John 4:20–21). Even though the first commandment (love of God)

1. Sider, *Living Like Jesus*, 32–34.
2. Harrington, *Interpreting*, 137.

and the second commandment (love of neighbor) are not the same thing, they cannot exist apart from one another.

Early High Christology

An examination of the first century world reveals a man named Jesus who preached a strange and beautiful message of hope to the world's disenfranchised masses. He was the Christ, the Messiah, the one foretold that would set at right the kingdom of God in the world. The early church emulated this Christ and took on the very characteristics of him during their ministry. As the body of Christ on earth, they reached out to the poor, the broken, the captives, the blind, and the bruised. Because of such emulations, the early believers were called Christians (like Christ) and the church existed in the world, reconciling it to the Father and being a blessing among the nations. The church today must understand that if the world is to recognize the church as Christ's body today, the church will have to emulate the characteristics of Christ among the very least, the very poor, and the stranger. It is when humanity sees the church being the church, a church that, like Christ, has God-like characteristics, they will accept Christ for themselves and glorify his Father which is in heaven. The point is summed up in the words of Jesus, "For I have given you an example, that ye should do as I have done to you" (John 13:15).

Modern Pentecostal Movements

Across South America the Pentecostal fires burn brighter and brighter each year (much like revivals throughout history). In 2006 the number of people claiming the Pentecostal experience in South America was one hundred and fifty-six million and the estimates today are well over two hundred million, while in North America they are approximately half of that. The North American church has not embraced the readily identifiable second commandment lessons embraced by the South American church. If programs, buildings, and money were the solution, the North American church would have remained, since its conception, vastly larger than its South American counterpart. However, sometimes with little or no money, Pentecostalism has exploded from the jungles of the Amazon to the craggy heights of the Andes Mountains and from the skyscrapers of Buenos Aries to the war-torn hamlets of El Salvador, past the wealthy

Christian armies of North America. While Pentecostals in North America are building bigger buildings and investing in higher education, in South America they are known for one thing, presenting the gospel in a frame that includes both loving God and loving neighbors. Somehow the church in North America must demonstrate that same kind of love for God by their love for others, instead of demonstrating their love for God with bigger and better things. When the joint-love commandment dwells together in North America, revival has and will explode at home in the same manner it has burst forth in other countries.

Summary of Section Two—Chapters 6–10

In Section One, we established the biblical precedent for living the second commandment. In Section Two, I have endeavored to demonstrate—through practical examples—how the second commandment looks in the community of the church. Pastoral care, often ignored and/or misunderstood in the life of the church, must start with an abiding love for God and neighbor (*chapter 6*). Instantaneous care/love for others will never happen spontaneously but is taught, or maybe caught, from the actions of others, where important education is demonstrated through community and fellowship (*chapter 7*). In a church community that still avoids counseling as if it were a plague, counseling, like education, may be more acceptable and desirable when demonstrated by the church, rather than found in the cold office of a therapist (*chapter 8*). Death has been increasingly and actively avoided by humanity and those that provide care. However, beauty can be found in one's last days when the overwhelming love of God is demonstrated by care providers that love their neighbors (*chapter 9*). We took a final look at one of the most pressing, and maybe governmentally unsolvable, problem of our time. While immigration is a growing problem for our world, a church that meets them with the love of the second commandment will find revival in places the church has not been able to reach (*chapter 10*).

Pastoral Care

No lesson could be more important than discovering that God's nature (his love and care for humanity) began with the creation of all things and continues throughout the biblical timeline. Biblical caregivers emulated the nature of God and/or God rebuked caregivers when they failed to provide the care his nature mandated. God required that his nature be demonstrated when care was provided by priests, prophets, and kings. Further, the biblical timeline connects God's nature, seen in the Old Testament, to the birth of the New Testament church: the creation of humanity in his image (Gen 1:26–28); the missional call of Abraham to bless the nations (Gen 12:1–3); the (re)circumcision of Israel by Joshua, linking them to the Mosaic Law and the Abrahamic Covenant (Josh 5); assuring the Babylonian diaspora of their restoration as God's people—including a shower of blessings for those gathered around the people of God (Ezek 36:26–31); commissioning the Christian diaspora to go and teach all nations (Matt 28:19); and the reminder to the early church that as the seed of Abraham, the heirs of his calling, and as followers of Jesus, they must emulate God's nature and live missionally as a blessing to all nations (Acts 3:25–26).

Such threads, seen throughout the biblical record, contain the core of God's mission—the restoration/redemption of humans as the image of God in the world. The Bible's command to "be a blessing" cannot be separated from the Great Commission—go and teach all nations—or from the great commandments: love God, love your neighbor. Ancient caregivers provided care in emulation of God's nature that was founded upon this foundation (be a blessing to all nations, go and teach all nations, and do so while loving God/loving others). The idea, that this heritage still exists today, remains the foundation on which all pastoral care must occur.

Education

The church's frustration over a lack of involvement and church growth, is magnified by the social issues found in every local community, and is ultimately the lack of a quality, educational experience. Unfortunately, the stand-up lecture style of most Christian education and self-help groups are one of the least effective education styles available, yet it seems to be the favorite of Christian educators everywhere. The hands-on experiential style of the second commandment allows for modeling Christian principles among the ministers/mentors/members in a manner that is more acceptable and/or understandable to all. Education demonstrated in love for others allows people, who never dreamed that they would, or even could, to become involved in the Christian educational process as both demonstrative teacher and recipient.

The church must become "a community capable of hearing the story of God we find in the Scripture and living in a manner that is faithful to that story."[3] When the church begins to live the second commandment in everyday life, Christian education will take place in more places than a church building. Christian education will then happen in the kitchen, the living room, the fellowship hall, the restaurant, the store, the barn, on a picnic, driving down the road, or at the mall. When this happens, the church will find that it has all the time and all the influence necessary to teach the vast number of topics needed to round out a mature Christian.

Counseling

Many Christians are in desperate need of quality marital counseling, and almost everyone needs supplemental support for their loneliness. Yet most don't know where to look or for what to ask. Even if they knew what they needed and were willing to ask for help, pride, self-image, and public perception prevents them from stepping forward for help. It is a shame that, for many, divorce holds less of a stigma than does counseling. Once again, this chapter shows that love for neighbor, demonstrated by those who love God, often fills this void. Men may be more likely to accept informal advice over a cup of coffee than they are to seek help while sitting on pastor's couch. Women are more likely to find help while attending a ladies' fellowship. Both are more open to exposure and assistance over a late-night game than sitting angrily together in pastor's office. Some are so lonely they would grasp ahold of any attention that would be sent their way: small children's Sunday School classes singing a few songs on a Saturday afternoon, youth classes on a scavenger hunt, or adults with a desire to fulfill Christ's command to love their neighbors.

Many counselees, while it may seem oversimplified, may only need help in meeting new friends to fill the empty loneliness that has consumed their lives. The amazing thing about the second commandment is that the lonely void, that is destroying the marriage of someone sitting on the church pew, could be filled by an outpouring of neighborly love for the lonely and forgotten of our neighborhoods. Time spent baking bread, shoveling their walk, and taking someone to the store (and eventually to church) could fill the hearts of the lonely with love and purpose that would spill over into their own life. In no time at all, those ministered to would

3. Foster, *Future*, 57.

begin to reciprocate with their own second commandment ministry to another neighbor down the street. Thus, revival is born!

Time of Death

The inherent Western aversion to death and dying, both of loved ones and strangers, prevents the opportunity to find beauty in the dying remnants of God's image. Little can be done to eliminate this cultural dislike of death, disease, and physical brokenness in the short-term. However, an abiding love for one's neighbor, powered by the overwhelming love of God, can push one through his/her repulsion for the visual and find beauty in the love demonstrated between the living and the dying. Those caring for the dying can step into this beauty by simply listening to their story, their last wishes, and assisting with unfinished business. The very presence of a caring/loving church builds community and affirms God's beauty in the lives of all his creation. Sometimes the less you say and the more you just *be there*, representing the God who loved the world while dying on the cross, is more beautiful than words can explain. When the church is there, the words of the cross still speak to the dying today, "Father, forgive them" (Luke 23:34), "Behold thy mother (son)" (John 19:26–27), and "Today shalt thou be with me" (Luke 23:43). Forgiveness, ongoing community, and the promise of eternal life is the demonstration of God's love for the very least (those that were killing him).

Immigration

The needs of 280.6 million immigrants are certainly in the minds of compassionate people everywhere, yet the overwhelming nature of their care needs inhibits practical research in real time. While many tears have been shed and many lessons learned by those who care, only a Spirit-inspired care response will enable today's church to navigate the vast differences in immigration stories, the broad array of their human/spiritual needs, and the setting of goals/outcomes that produce the best long-term results. This inability to unravel the many *unknowns* and the *otherness* associated with intercultural care, can only be mitigated by a church that loves them as they do themselves, welcomes them as Christ did the outcasts of his time, and builds a new community together that looks more like the first church. Since "Pentecostals are comfortable with emergent, affective, and nonlinear processes of change in which the Holy Spirit acts and people follow,"[4] they are better suited to care for the migrant people that arrive daily.

Final Thoughts

Finally, this book has developed a definition for second commandment ministry: *"When exposed by proximity to need, the second commandment is a command to practically demonstrate one's love for his/her neighbor(s), down to the least of them, loving them as one does him/herself, thus indicating the depth of one's love for God."* The elements of this definition, proximity and practical love to the least of our world, demonstrate to our broken world, and more importantly to God, the depth and height of one's love for Jesus Christ, the Redeemer. This definition is mirrored in the first and second great commandments of Jesus, "Thou shalt love the Lord thy God with all thy heart, and with all thy soul, and with all thy mind. This is the first and great commandment. And the second *is* like unto it, Thou shalt love thy neighbor as thyself. On these two commandments hang all the law and the prophets" (Matt 22:36–40; Mark 12:28–34; Luke10:35–37). The fitting, final words of this book come from the mouth of our Lord to all, "Go and do likewise" (Luke 10:37).

4. Myers, *Progressive Pentecostalism*, 119.

Bibliography

Adams, Jay E. *Competent to Counsel: Introduction to Nouthetic Counseling.* Grand Rapids, MI: Zondervan, 1986.

Aden, Leroy. "Comfort/Sustaining." In *Dictionary of Pastoral Care and Counseling*, edited by Rodney J. Hunter and Nancy J. Ramsay, 193–95. Nashville, TN: Abingdon, 2005.

Anderson, Ray S. *The Shape of Practical Theology: Empowering Ministry with Theological Praxis.* Downers Grove, IL: InterVarsity, 2001.

Anthony, Michael J., ed. *Introducing Christian Education: Foundations for the Twenty-1st Century.* Grand Rapids, MI: Baker, 2001.

Baker, Jim, and Ken Abraham. *The Refuge: A Look into the Future and the Power of Living in a Christian Community.* Nashville, TN: Thomas Nelson, 2000.

Barna, George. *Growing True Disciples; New Strategies for Producing Genuine Followers of Christ.* Colorado Springs: Water Brook, 2001.

Bastian, Jean Pierre. "The New Religious Map of Latin America: Causes and Social Effects." *Cross Currents* 48, no. 3 (Fall 1998) 330–46.

Benner, David G. *Strategic Pastoral Counseling; a Short-term Structured Model.* Grand Rapids, MI: Baker, 1992.

Bennett, Joyce N. "'I Became More Maya': International Kaqchikel Maya Migration in Central America." *Universitas Psychologica* 16, no. 5 (2017) 1–13.

Benson, Warren S. "Philosophical Foundations of Christian Education." In *Introducing Christian Education: Foundations for the Twenty-1st Century*, edited by Michael J. Anthony, 18–26. Grand Rapids, MI: Baker, 2001.

Berends, Kurt O. "Social Variables and Community Response." In *Pentecostal Currents in American Protestantism*, edited by Edith Blumhofer, Grant A. Walker, Grant Walker, and Russell P. Spittler, 68–89. Chicago, IL: University of Illinois Press, 1999.

Bernard, David K. *Growing a Church.* Hazelwood, MO: Word Aflame, 2001.

Blumhofer, Edith L. *Restoring the Faith; The Assemblies of God, Pentecostalism, and American Culture.* Chicago, IL: University of Illinois Press, 1993.

Boone, R. Jerome. "Community and Worship: The Key Components of Pentecostal Christian Formation." *Flowers Heritage Center* (1994) 243–79.

Bromiley, Geoffrey W., ed. *The International Standard Bible Encyclopedia, Vol. 3*. Grand Rapids, MI: Eerdmans, 1986.

Burck, J. Russell. "Community, Fellowship, and Care." In *Dictionary of Pastoral Care and Counseling*, edited by Rodney J. Hunter and Nancy J. Ramsay, 202–03. Nashville, TN: Abingdon, 2005.

Burfield, David R. "Identifying Pastoral Care in Contemporary Methodism." PhD diss., University of Nottingham, 1995.

Butrin, J. *From the Roots Up: A Closer Look at Compassion and Justice in Mission*. Springfield, MO: Roots UP, 2010.

Campbell, Alistair. *Professionalism and Pastoral Care*. Philadelphia, PA: Fortress, 1985.

Carroll (Rodas), M. Daniel. *Christians at the Border: Immigration, the Church, and the Bible*. 2nd ed. Grand Rapids, MI: Brazos, 2013.

Chuga, R. I. "The Wholistic Ministry of the Church in the Twenty-First Century." *Baptist Theological Seminary Kaduna* 1, no. 1 (April 2005) 4–16.

Ciampa, Ralph C. "God-Talk in Pastoral Care: Three Dimensions of the Pastoral Encounter." Paper presented at the Cumberland, Maryland Memorial Hospital, 1994.

Clark, Robert E., Lin Johnson, and Allyn K. Sloat, eds. *Christian Education: Foundations for the Future*. Chicago, IL: Moody, 1991.

Clinebell, Howard J. *Basic Types of Pastoral Care and Counseling: Resources for the Ministry of Healing and Growth*, 3rd ed. Edited by Howard J. Clinebell, Jr. and Bridget Clare McKeever. Nashville, TN: Abingdon, 2011.

Collins, Gary R. *The Biblical Basis of Christian Counseling for People Helpers*. Colorado Springs, CO: NavPress, 2001.

———. *The Biblical Basis of Christian Counseling; Meeting Counseling Needs Through the Local Church*. Colorado Springs, CO: NavPress, 2001.

Comiskey, Joel. *Leadership Explosion: Multiplying Cell Group Leaders to Reap the Harvest*. Houston, TX: Touch, 2000.

Corbett, Steve, and Brian Fikkert. *When Helping Hurts: How to Alleviate Poverty Without Hurting the Poor . . . and Yourself*. Chicago: Moody, 2014.

Crossan, John D. "The Life of a Mediterranean Jewish Peasant." *Christian Century* 108 (1991): 1194–1200.

Culbertson, Philip L. *Caring for God's People: Counseling and Christian Wholeness*. Minneapolis, MN: Fortress, 2006.

Dayton, Donald W. *Theological Roots of Pentecostalism*. Peabody, MA: Hendrickson, 1987.

Deeks, David. *Pastoral Theology: An Inquiry*. London, UK: Epworth, 1987.

Dempster, Murray, et al., eds. *The Globalization of Pentecostalism: A Religion Made to Travel*. Eugene, OR: Wipf & Stock, 2011.

DeSpelder, Lynn Ann, and Albert Lee Strickland. *The Last Dance: Encountering Death and Dying*. Mountain View, CA: Mayfield, 2019.

Dockery, David S., and David P. Gushee. *The Future of Christian Higher Education*. Nashville, TN: Broadman & Holman, 1999.

Doehring, Carrie. *The Practice of Pastoral Care, Revised and Expanded Edition: A Postmodern Approach*. Louisville, KY: Westminster John Knox, 2015.

Doty, Lynda A. *Apostolic Counseling; Helping God's People God's Way*. Kearney, NE: Morris, 2000.

Downey, Glanville. "Who is My Neighbor? The Greek and Roman Answer." *Anglican Theological Review* 47 (1965) 3–15.

Downs, Perry G. *Teaching for Spiritual Growth: An Introduction to Christian Education.* Grand Rapids, MI: Zondervan, 1994.

Dube, Musa W. "Theological Challenges: Proclaiming the Fullness of Life in the HIV/AIDS & Global Economic Era." *International Review of Mission* 91 (2002) 535–49.

Ellison, Jessie. "Lewiston, Maine, Revived by Somali Immigrants." *Newsweek.* (January 16, 2009). http://www.newsweek.com/lewiston-maine-revived-somali-immigrants-78475.

Elmer, Duane. *Cross-Cultural Servanthood: Serving the World in Christlike Humility.* Downers Grove, IL: IVP Academic, 2006.

Ewart, Frank J. *The Phenomenon of Pentecost.* Hazelwood, MO: Word Aflame, 1947.

Flemming, Dean. *Recovering the Full Mission of God: A Biblical Perspective on Being, Doing and Telling.* Downers Grove, IL: IVP Academic, 2013.

Foster, Charles R. *The Future of Christian Education: Educating Congregations.* Nashville, TN: Abingdon, 1994.

Frazee, Randy. *The Connecting Church; Beyond Small Groups to Authentic Community.* Grand Rapids, MI: Zondervan, 2001.

French, Talmadge L. *Our God is One: The Story of the Oneness Pentecostals.* Indianapolis, IN: Voice and Vision, 1999.

Furnish, Victor Paul. "Love of Neighbor in the New Testament." *Journal of Religious Ethics* 10 (1982) 327–34.

Gerkin, Charles V. "Interpretation and Hermeneutics, Pastoral." In *Dictionary of Pastoral Care and Counseling,* edited by Rodney J. Hunter and Nancy J. Ramsay, 591–93. Nashville, TN: Abingdon, 2005.

———. *An Introduction to Pastoral Care.* Nashville, TN: Abingdon, 1997.

Getz, Gene A. *Building Up One Another: How Every Member of the Church Can Help Strengthen Other Christians.* Wheaton, IL: Victor, 1976.

Graham, Larry Kent. "Healing." In *Dictionary of Pastoral Care and Counseling,* edited by Rodney J. Hunter and Nancy J. Ramsay, 497–501. Nashville, TN: Abingdon Press, 2005.

Grant, Beth. *Courageous Compassion: Confronting Social Injustice God's way.* Springfield, MO: My Healthy Church, 2014.

Harrington, Daniel J. *Interpreting the New Testament: A Practical Guide.* Collegeville, MN: Liturgical, 1990.

Hartung, John. "Love Thy Neighbor: The Evolution of In-Group Morality," *Skeptic* 3, no. 4 (1995) 86–99.

Hasell, Joe. "From $1.90 to $2.15: the updated International Poverty Line." *DoSomething. org.* https://www.dosomething.org/us/facts/11-facts-about-global-poverty.

Hobson, George. *Imago Dei: Man/Woman Created in the Image of God: Implications for Theology, Pastoral Care, Eucharist, Apologetics, Aesthetics.* Eugene, OR: Wipf & Stock, 2019.

Hoekema, Anthony A. *Created in God's image.* Grand Rapids, MI: Eerdmans, 1994.

Homrighausen, Elmer G. "Who is My Neighbor? The Christian and the Non-Christian." *Interpretations* 4, no. 4 (October 1950): 401–15.

Hopkins, Gerald Manley. *Poems and Prose.* Edited by W. H. Gardner. London, UK: Penguin, 1963.

Horton, Stanley M., ed. *Systematic Theology.* Springfield, MO: Logion, 2007.

Hughes, Selwyn. *Every Day Light.* Nashville, TN: Broadman & Holman, 1997.

Hunter, Rodney J., and Nancy J. Ramsay, eds. *Dictionary of Pastoral Care and Counseling.* Nashville, TN: Abingdon, 2005.

Hutchison, Owen. *Christian Love in Everyday Living.* Philadelphia, PA: Westminster, 1955.

Im, Chandler H., and Amos Yong, eds. *Global Diasporas and Mission: Regnum Edinburgh Centenary, Vol. 23.* Eugene, OR: Wipf & Stock, 2014.

Janse van Rensburg, J. "A Holistic Approach to Pastoral Care and Poverty." *Verbum et Ecclesia* 31, no. 1 (January 2010.) 1–7.

Johnson, Eric L., ed. *Foundations for Soul Care: A Christian Psychology Proposal.* Downers Grove, IL: IVP Academic, 2014.

Justes, Emma J. *Hearing Beyond the Words: How to Become a Listening Pastor.* Nashville, TN: Abingdon, 2006.

Kazen, Thomas. "The Christology of Early Christian Practice," *Journal of Biblical Literature* 127 (2008) 591–614.

Kellemen, Robert W. *Gospel Conversations: How to Care Like Christ: Equipping Biblical Counselors.* Grand Rapids, MI: Zondervan, 2015.

Keller, Timothy. *Generous Justice: How God's Grace Makes Us Just.* New York, NY: Penguin, 2010.

Lane, Belden C. *Ravished by Beauty: The Surprising Legacy of Reformed Spirituality.* Oxford: Oxford University Press, 2011.

Larson-Miller, Lizette. "Caring for the Sick: A Historical Overview of a Central Ministry of the Church," *Liturgical Ministry* 16, no. 4 (2007) 172–80.

Lartey, Emmanuel Y. *Pastoral Theology in an Intercultural World.* Eugene, OR: Wipf & Stock Publishers, 2013.

Lawson, Kevin E. "Historical Foundations of Christian Education." In *Introducing Christian Education: Foundations for the Twenty-first Century,* edited by Michael J. Anthony, 17–28. Grand Rapids, MI: Baker, 2001.

McClung Jr., L. Grant. *Azusa Street and Beyond: Pentecostal Missions and Church Growth in the Twentieth Century.* South Plainfield, NJ: Bridge, 1986.

Migration Data Portal. "Diasporas." Geneva, Switzerland: International Organization for Migration. https://migrationdataportal.org/themes/diasporas.

Migration Data Portal. https://www.migrationdataportal.org/international-data?i=stock_abs_&t=2020.

Mitchell, Kenneth R. "Guidance, Pastoral." In *Dictionary of Pastoral Care and Counseling,* edited by Rodney J. Hunter and Nancy J. Ramsay, 486–87. Nashville, TN: Abingdon, 2005.

Moore, T. M. "The Hope of Beauty in an Age of Ugliness and Death." *Theology Today* 61 (2004) 155–72.

Morales, Gamaliel Lugo. "Moving Forward with the Latin American Pentecostal Movement." *International Review of Mission* 87 (October 1988) 504–12.

Myers, Bryant L. "Progressive Pentecostalism, Development, and Christian Development NGOs: A Challenge and an Opportunity." *International Bulletin of Missionary Research* 39, no. 3 (July 2015) 115–20.

Neudecker, Reinhard. "And You Shall Love Your Neighbor as Yourself—I Am the Lord. Lev. 19:18 in Jewish Interpretation." *Biblica* 73 (1992) 496–517.

Neuger, Christie Cozad. *Counseling Women: A Narrative, Pastoral Approach.* Minneapolis, MN: Fortress, 2001.

Niswonger, Richard. *New Testament History.* Grand Rapids, MI: Zondervan, 1988.

O'Donohue, John. *Beauty: The Invisible Embrace.* New York, NY: Harper Perennial, 2005.

Oxford Online Dictionary, *s.v.* "Emotions." https://en.oxforddictionaries.com/definition/emotion.

Oxford Online Dictionary, *s.v.* "Physical." https://en.oxforddictionaries.com/definition/physical.

Oxford Online Dictionary, *s.v.* "Relational." https://en.oxforddictionaries.com/definition/relational.

Patterson, Stephen J. "Why the Historical Jesus?" *Living Pulpit* 3 (1994) 20–21.

Pazmino, Robert W. *Foundational Issues in Christian Education: An Introduction in Evangelical Perspective*. Grand Rapids, MI: Baker, 1997.

Peck, M. Scott. *The Different Drum: Community Making and Peace*. New York, NY: Simon & Schuster, 1987.

Pew Research Report. "Faith on the Move: The Religious Affiliation of International Migrants." http://www.pewforum.org/2012/03/08/religious-migration-exec/.

Peyton, Joey R. "Finding a Place of Beauty: Providing Pastoral Care at the Time of Death." DMin diss., Eden Theological Seminary (Webster University), 2013.

———. "A Modern Exodus in Need of Care: Holistic Pastoral Care to Diaspora Populations in the St. Louis, Missouri, Area." PhD diss., Assembly of God Theological Seminary, 2022.

Rahner, Karl. *The Love of Jesus and the Love of Neighbor*. New York, NY: Crossroads, 1983.

Richmond, Mary E. *The Good Neighbor in the Modern City*. Philadelphia, PA: Lippincott, 1907.

Rickerson, Wayne. "Building Healthy Families." In *Christian Education: Foundations for the Future*, edited by Robert E. Clark, Lin Johnson, and Allyn K. Sloat, 575. Chicago, IL: Moody, 1991.

Robinson, Haddon. *Biblical Preaching: The Development and Delivery of Expository Messages*. Grand Rapids, MI: Baker, 2001.

Scheib, Karen D. *Pastoral Care: Telling the Stories of Our Lives*. Nashville, TN: Abingdon, 2016.

Self, Charlie. *Flourishing Churches & Communities: A Pentecostal Primer on Faith, Work, and Economics for Spirit-Empowered Discipleship*. Grand Rapids, MI: Christian's Library, 2013.

Sharp, Melinda McGarrah. *Creating Resistances: Pastoral Care in a Postcolonial World*. Boston, MA: Brill, 2019.

Sider, Ronald J. *Living Like Jesus*. Grand Rapids, MI: Baker, 1996.

Slaughter, James R. "Biblical Perspectives for the Family." In *Christian Education: Foundations for the Future*, edited by Robert E. Clark, Lin Johnson, and Allyn K. Sloat, 567. Chicago, IL: Moody, 1991.

Snyder, Susanna. *Asylum-Seeking, Migration and Church (Explorations in Practical, Pastoral and Empirical Theology)*. New York, NY: Routledge, 2016.

Soerens, Matthew, and Jenny Hwang Yang. *Welcoming the Stranger: Justice, Compassion, and Truth in the Immigration Debate*. Downers Grove, IL: InterVarsity, 2009.

Spence, H. D. M., ed. *The Pulpit Commentary, vol. 16*. Grand Rapids, MI: Eerdmans, 1950.

Stewart, Charles W. *The Minister as Marriage Counselor; a Role-relationship Theory of Marital Counseling and Pastoral Care*. New York, NY: Abingdon, 1961.

Swedenborg, Emanuel. *Charity: The Practice of Neighborliness*. West Chester, PA: Swedenborg Foundation, 1995.

Swidler, Leonard. "The Jewishness of Jesus: Some Religious Implications for Christians." *Journal of Ecumenical Studies* 18 (1981) 104–13.

Synan, Vinson. *Century of the Holy Spirit; 100 years of Pentecostal and Charismatic Renewal, 1901–2001*. Nashville, TN: Thomas Nelson, 2001.

———. *The Holiness-Pentecostal Movement in the United States*. Grand Rapids, MI: Eerdmans, 1971.

Taussig, Hal. *In the Beginning Was the Meal: Social Experimentation and Early Christian Identity*. Minneapolis, MN: Fortress, 2009.

Taylor, Nick. "Spiritual Formation: Nurturing Spiritual Vitality." In *Introducing Christian Education: Foundations for the Twenty-first Century*, edited by Michael J. Anthony, 91–100. Grand Rapids, MI: Baker, 2001.

Tertullian, Apology 3, quoted by Pagels, Elaine. *Beyond Belief: The Secret Gospel of Thomas*. New York, NY: Random, 2003.

Thornton, Sharon. *Broken Yet Beloved: A Pastoral Theology of the Cross*. St. Louis, MO: Chalice, 2002.

Van Gelder, Craig. *The Essence of the Church*. Grand Rapids, MI: Baker, 2000.

Wacker, Grant. *Heaven Below: Early Pentecostals and American Culture*. Cambridge, MA: Harvard University Press, 2003.

Wallace, Mary H. *Profiles of Pentecostal Preachers, Volume I*. Hazelwood, MO: Word Aflame, 1983.

———. *Profiles of Pentecostal Preachers, Volume II*. Hazelwood, MO: Word Aflame, 1984.

Walqui, Aida. "Contextual Factors in 2nd Language Acquisition." November 6, 2000.

Wan, Enoch, and Sadiri Joy Tira. *Missions Practice in the 21st Century*. Pasadena, CA: William Carey International University Press, 2009.

Wellmeier, Nancy J. "Santa Eulalia's People in Exile: Maya Religion, Culture, and Identity in Los Angeles." In *Gatherings in Diaspora: Religious Communities and the New Immigration*, edited by R. Stephen Warner and Judith G. Wittner, 97–122. Philadelphia, PA: Temple University Press, 1998.

Wilhoit, James C., and John M. Dettoni, eds. *Nuture That is Christian: Developmental Perspectives on Christian Educations*. Grand Rapids, MI: Baker, 1995.

Wilken, Robert L. *The Christians as the Romans Saw Them*. 2nd ed. New Haven, CT: Yale University Press, 2003.

Wise, Carrol A. *The Meaning of Pastoral Care*. New York, NY: Harper & Row, 1966.

Wright, Christopher J. H. *The Mission of God: Unlocking the Bible's Grand Narrative*. Downers Grove, IL: IVP Academic, 2018.

Printed in the USA
CPSIA information can be obtained
at www.ICGtesting.com
LVHW011544080324
773936LV00040B/903

9 781666 788204